THE DOCTRiNE of REPROBATION in the CHRiSTiAN REFORMED CHURCH

HARRY R. BOER

GRAND RAPIDS, MICHIGAN
WILLIAM B. EERDMANS PUBLISHING COMPANY

Copyright ©1983 by William B. Eerdmans Publishing Company
255 Jefferson Ave. S.E., Grand Rapids, Michigan 49503

Library of Congress Cataloging in Publication Data

Boer, Harry R.
   The doctrine of reprobation in the Christian
Reformed Church.

   1. Reprobation—History of doctrines—20th century.
2. Christian Reformed Church—Doctrinal and controversial
works. 3. Boer, Harry R. I. Title.
BT809.B63 1983   234   83-1602
ISBN 0-8028-1952-4

CONTENTS

WHY THIS BOOK WAS WRITTEN

The doctrine of reprobation is an evaded and embarrassing religious and theological reality in the Christian Reformed Church. In the doctrine of predestination, reprobation is the dark and sinister face, while election is the bright and shining face. The question that will not go away is how the God and Father of our Lord Jesus Christ can manifest himself through the sinister as well as through the shining face. The official teaching of the church is that both faces together equally, eternally, and absolutely reveal the being of God. Through them God "manifest[s] Himself such as He is; that is to say, merciful and just"; merciful through election, just through reprobation (Belgic Confession, Article XVI). The elect are saved and glorified "for the demonstration of His mercy, and for the praise of the riches of His glorious grace"; the reprobate are condemned and punished "for the declaration of His justice" (Canons of Dort I/7, 15). Just as election takes place without regard to any merit in the elect, so reprobation takes place without regard to any demerit in the reprobate. Both election and reprobation take place according to God's sovereign "good pleasure."

Such is "that decree of election and reprobation, revealed in the Word of God, which, though men of perverse, impure, and unstable minds wrest it to their own destruction, yet to holy and pious souls affords unspeakable consolation" (Canons I/6).

These two inseparable doctrines constitute the cornerstone of the Christian Reformed credal structure. They determine the character of the Canons of Dort as a whole, which in turn form the standard whereby the relevant teachings of the Belgic Confession and the Heidelberg Catechism are to be understood (Form of Subscription, *Psalter Hymnal*, Doctrinal Standards, p. 71).

The Form of Subscription, the signing of which is incumbent on all office-bearers in the Christian Reformed Church and all professors of Calvin College and Seminary, includes the affirmation that the teachings of the creeds "do fully agree with the Word of God." Those who sign the Forms thus commit themselves "diligently to teach and faithfully to defend" the doctrine of reprobation. In actuality, no teaching in the credal panoply of doctrines is more ignored, suppressed, and enveloped in silence, disregard, and neglect than this doctrine. Why, then, should we be disturbed about its existence? Why not write it off as an anti-quated piece of rationlistic theology long since left behind?

We can make no greater mistake than to view the role of reprobation in Christian Reformed theological and religious think-ing in this way. While not active in theological expression and pastoral practice, it is dynamically alive in the prudential mind of the church. No Christian Reformed minister or professor dares to write about election with the open assertion that there is no such thing as reprobation. None dares to repudiate the doctrine. None dares to say that it impugns God's holiness, love, sincerity, and redemptive concern for the whole of humankind. When the Reverend Harold Dekker, Professor of Missions at Calvin Theological Seminary, clearly implied just this in the *Reformed Journal* in December 1962 and February 1963, he unleashed a storm that did not blow itself out until a synodical decision in 1967, which settled nothing, gave all concerned to understand that the doctrine of reprobation sets limits not only to the efficacy of the gospel but also to Christian Reformed freedom of theological expression.

In 1977 I submitted to the synod of the CRC an official objec-tion to the doctrine of reprobation, challenging its validity. My aim was to show that the Scriptures that are officially adduced to establish the teaching of reprobation in the Canons of Dort do not in fact do so; further, I requested that therefore the doc-trine be "exscinded from or become a non-binding part of the creeds of the Christian Reformed Church." The synod appointed a nine-man study committee to evaluate the objection and report to the Synod of 1980.

This book tells the story of the theological argumentation and the ecclesiastical procedures that led to the unqualified rejection of my petition by the Synod of 1980 and the reaffirmation of that rejection by the Synod of 1981. The story that I have to relate is not an edifying one. In adopting without reservation the report of the three-year study committee and commending it to the churches as an "elucidation" of the teaching of the Canons on election and reprobation, the synod attributed meanings to this teaching that are theologically wholly alien to that carefully crafted creed. In the synodical position reprobation ceases to have its own decretal status and becomes instead an "aspect" or "facet" of the decree of election. There appears to be no connection between God's eternal decree to pass some people by with his grace and the punishment of eternal death that will be pronounced upon them in the last judgment. Crucial statements in Canons I/15 (the classic statement of reprobation) receive either no attention or distorted attention in the report. The far-reaching significance of the literary structure of Canons I/6 and I/15 is wholly ignored. The report finds the decree of election, on which the whole of its theological case rests, a very imperfect doctrine at best. At the close of its argumentation, by an undeniably clear implication it concedes the central thrust of the objection to reprobation. In the course of these expositions God is made the "deficient cause of unbelief"—in contradiction of the Canon's clear statement that God is "in no wise" the cause of unbelief. Quite appropriately, in the pastoral section of the report the word reprobation is in two headings printed as "Reprobation" whereas election in two corresponding headings is printed Election—without quotation marks. And last, but certainly not least, the traditional basis for the doctrine of reprobation is declared invalid, and in its place has come a new scriptural substratum for a doctrine of "limited election."

The questionable character of the study committee report is fully paralleled by the impropriety of the manner in which the synod acted upon it. Eight weeks after the report appeared in the Agenda the Synod of 1980 adopted it. Yet the church as a whole had no inkling of what it contained, nor had the members of synod seen it before the long and complex document appeared in the Agenda. Chapter 4 sets forth in some detail not only the impropriety but the crass illegality of this action, and also the highly peculiar endorsement of this procedure by the Synod of 1981.

It is, I believe, by no means without significance that as of this writing (December 1982) no meaningful exposition of or commentary on the new Christian Reformed teaching on reprobation has appeared in public print. The historic silence and evasiveness with respect to the incriminated doctrine remains in full effect. This, for a denomination that claims to have a particularly insightful understanding of the "full counsel of God," is not a matter of praise.

Consistories, classes, and synods are the appointed stewards
of the creeds of the church. But they are *stewards* of them, not
owners who may or may not let the church, the true owner, know
how they have changed their meaning. This book is therefore
written for the church. It is written for the theologically un-
schooled laity as well as for ministers and professors. The creeds
belong to the church as a body of believers, and the Bible was
not written for academics but for that same body of the faithful.
Therefore theology as reflection on the faith that the church confesses must address that same body. If you who have this book
in hand are of clear mind, cherish the well-being of Christ's
church, and have appropriated its pastoral instruction, you should
be able to read it with understanding. If you who have this book
in hand are learned in theology as a minister or as a professor
of theology or otherwise, I invite you to apply your keenest
thought and analysis to it, for the subject is large and needs the
counsel of the wise as well as the understanding of the un-
sophisticated.

The doctrine of reprobation, openly incriminated from 1977
to 1980, was quickly and furtively vindicated by an uncomprehending synod and then, by general consent, reconsigned to the
limbo of disregard as the favorite Christian Reformed manner
of "confessing" it. Since we choose so to "hold' the doctrine,
belief in which is alleged to bless the pious with "unspeakable
consolation," we cannot but ask whether this state of affairs may
be permitted to continue.

With this as introduction, I invite you to read the story.

—**Harry R. Boer**

CHAPTER 1

HISTORY OF A CONCERN

My concern with the doctrine of reprobation as a religious, theological, and ecclesiastical problem in the Christian Reformed Church (CRC) has a long history. Already in 1963 I felt that the time for official action had come, and I prepared a statement for submission to the synod requesting its excision from the creed of the church. When it was ready to be sent in, however, I judged it better not to submit it, at least not at that time. A controversy of major proportions had arisen in the CRC occasioned by articles published in the *Reformed Journal* by Harold Dekker, professor of missionary theology at Calvin Theological Seminary. The title of his first article set forth the central issue: "God so Loved— All Men." Its import was that God loved all men redemptively, not only a certain segment of the human race known as the elect. It aroused severe criticism and led to extended ecclesiastical concern involving consistories, classes, and synods.

Professor Dekker and I were college and seminary classmates as well as friends. I feared that my protest against the doctrine of reprobation would be viewed by many as a political device to divert pressure from him. Fourteen years were to elapse before I again prepared an address to synod. If this seems a long time to delay execution of my resolve to protest officially, it is nevertheless true that I did not delay further action by so much as one day beyond what was necessary.

There were important reasons for this delay. Obviously, the "Love of God controversy," as the Dekker case came to be known, had first to run its course. It was concluded by a highly ambiguous adjudication in 1967. By that time there had been such an exercise of ecclesiastical procedures, doctrinal and exegetical opinion, and emotional concern that an immediate continuation of substantially the same issue, albeit in different ecclesiastical and theological format, seemed unwise. Meanwhile, in the midst of a missionary furlough in 1964, I was invited to address the faculty and students of Calvin Theological Seminary on a mission subject of my choosing. It seemed appropriate to address the question of reprobation from a missionary point of view. I spoke on "Reprobation and the Preaching of the Gospel." The preparation and delivery of this address persuaded me anew of the urgency of facing this problem, as well as of its relevance to the controversy centering about Professor Dekker, which was then growing apace in scope and seriousness. I therefore published this lecture in two articles in the March and April issues of the *Reformed Journal* (1965).

In June of that year, having returned to Nigeria, I received a strong protest from the consistory of the First Christian Reformed Church in Roseland, Chicago, my calling church, against the publication of these articles. I had violated the requirements of the Form of Subscription; I was to cease all speaking, writing, or teaching respecting the expressed sentiments, and to give a further explanation of my views so that the consistory might judge them. (In May I had received notice from another consistory that it would call me to account at the next classical assembly.)

It perplexed me much that both Professor Dekker and I, speaking out of missionary concern, could be so set upon by the official ecclesiastical organization. The basis for these attacks on our freedom of expression was clear. It was the Form of Subscription.[1] We were alleged, each in his own context, to have spoken beyond the limits set for office-bearers in the CRC. In a meeting with my consistory during my next furlough in 1968, I requested them to inform me officially of the scriptural basis for the doctrine of reprobation. This was refused on the ground that it could be done only in response to an official protest addressed to the church. I appealed to Classis Chicago South to inform me of the scriptural basis in question, and I received the same reply.

Since both my consistory and my classis urged me to resort to the official process, and I had all along intended to do so at the first opportunity, why did I continue to hold off? Driven by the experienced realities of church life, I had made a careful study of the Form of Subscription. In that study I discovered that under its terms the process of credal revision on which I was urged to embark was thoroughly repugnant to the Reformed understanding

1. A declaration affirming unreserved agreement with the teachings of the three creeds of the CRC, which must be signed by all office-bearers of the CRC and by all teachers of Calvin College and Seminary before they can enter upon their official duties. It can be found on page 71 in the section on Doctrinal Standards in the back of the Christian Reformed *Psalter Hymnal*.

of the character of the church. The process of weighing the merits of my protest would in every respect be a thoroughly hierarchical affair in which the members of the church as a whole would be voiceless so far as support of change was concerned. Speech in favor of change could only be made in the assembly handling the protest. Even the most knowledgeable theologians, if they were not members of the adjudicating assembly, would have to be publicly silent if they were in support of change. On the other hand, anyone who wished to oppose change openly was free to do so. When everything had been decided by the synod, then and only then would the church be informed of the revision, if any, that had been effected in the content of its faith.

In Roman Catholic teaching the church is divided into two parts, the hierarchy and the laity. More formally, they are known as the *ecclesia docens* (the teaching church) and the *ecclesia audiens* (the hearing church). The *ecclesia docens* teaches and governs, the *ecclesia audiens* hears, believes, and obeys. In all essentials this is the way in which the Synod of Dort, 1618-19, conceived of the government of the church on the score of credal revision when it drew up the Form of Subscription, which remained unrevised in the CRC until 1976. But this is quite intolerable in a Reformed framework. True, only the synod can make an official decision on credal revision. But the church membership and the church's theologians should be able to engage in public discussion of proposed changes deeply affecting the faith and life of the church. The creeds do not belong to a hierarchic assembly of clergy and elders, but to the body of believers. Since I did not wish to enter into a process of credal revision that wholly excluded the church, I declined all advice that I should officially protest the church's teaching of the doctrine of reprobation.

It thus became clear that what was needed was a revision of the Form of Subscription. In 1970, therefore, I published a series of nine articles in the *Reformed Journal* criticizing the existing provisions governing the process of revision in terms of history, Scripture, and the Reformed conception of the church. Having done so, I expected that somewhere someone would pick up the cause and transform the argument into an overture to synod requesting revision. But nothing happened. So I wrote an overture myself. This effort was well supported by a similar overture from the Evergreen Park, Chicago, Christian Reformed church.

The Synod of 1974 acted affirmatively on these overtures by appointing a study committee, which reported favorably to the Synod of 1976. This concern led to two fundamental enactments providing that

> . . . when the constituted synod declares the matter [i.e., the official protest] to be legally before it for action, all signers of the Form of Subscription shall be free to discuss it with the whole church until adjudicated by synod.

and

> A revision of the confessions shall not be adopted by synod until the whole church membership shall have had adequate opportunity to consider it.[2]

In making this decision synod agreed that in the event that any future synod should be called upon to revise the creed, the delegates should be informed not only by their own study but also by study and discussion in the fellowship of the church as a whole. In short, credal revision had now become a matter of direct concern to the church in its entirety. The synodical enactments in question were the more weighty because they were not simply synodical legislation but were accorded Church Order status. No small part of the educational purpose that this present book may serve will be to note the non-role that these important Church Order revisions played at the synods of 1980 and 1981.

The same synod (1976), presumably because of general knowledge of my difficulties with the consistory of my calling church, generously permitted me "to submit a confessional revision gravamen . . . directly to synod." The ground it gave for this was the "long and intricate history of the matter." After thirteen years of study, writing, concern, and ecclesiastical unpleasantness, and finding support at long last in a piece of basic reform in the church, I was finally in position to submit an address to synod against the doctrine of reprobation on a solid ecclesiastical basis. My gravamen was in the hands of the Stated Clerk by March 1977, and three months later it lay on the synodical table for action.

* * *

Before proceeding with the history that followed the submission of my address to the synod, it will be good to clarify three matters.

2. *Acts of Synod*, 1976, pp. 69, 70.

One is: What is a gravamen? The second is: What are the credal statements to which my protest took exception? And third: What do we mean by "reprobation"?

In order not to confuse the reader I have up to this point spoken of an "address" or "protest" that in due time I submitted to the synod of the Christian Reformed Church. The official term to designate such an address or protest is "gravamen," which I shall use from here on. It is derived from the Latin word *gravis* meaning heavy, weighty, burdensome, serious. The English words grave, gravity, and gravitation come from it. In Reformed church law a gravamen is an *official objection* to an *official teaching* of the church. It is normally submitted to a synod via ecclesiastical channels and, when accepted for action, requires the synod *to examine* it and to express *a judgment* upon it.

The second matter of which we must take note concerns the credal statements against which the gravamen was directed. These were taken from two articles in the First Head of Doctrine of the Canons of Dort.

Article 6

That some receive the gift of faith from God, and others do not receive it, proceeds from God's eternal decree. *For known unto God are all his works from the beginning of the world* (Acts 15:18, A.V.). *Who worketh all things after the counsel of his will* (Eph. 1:11). According to which decree He graciously softens the hearts of the elect, however obstinate, and inclines them to believe; while He leaves the non-elect in His just judgment to their own wickedness and obduracy. And herein is especially displayed the profound, the merciful, and at the same time the righteous discrimination between men equally involved in ruin; or that decree of election and reprobation, revealed in the Word of God, which, though men of perverse, impure, and unstable minds wrest it to their own destruction, yet to holy and pious souls affords unspeakable consolation.

Article 15

What peculiarly tends to illustrate and recommend to us the eternal and unmerited grace of election is the express testimony of sacred Scripture that not all, but some only, are elected, while others are passed by in the eternal decree; whom God, out of His sovereign, most just, irreprehensible, and unchangeable good pleasure, has decreed to leave in the common misery into which they have wilfully plunged themselves, and not to bestow upon them saving faith and the grace of conversion; but, permitting them in His just judgment to follow their own ways, at last, for the declaration of His justice, to condemn and punish them forever, not only on account of their unbelief, but also for all their other sins. And this is the decree of reprobation, which by no means makes God the Author of sin (the very thought of which is blasphemy), but declares Him to be an awful, irreprehensible, and righteous Judge and Avenger thereof.

The gravamen makes no mention of Article XVI in the Belgic Confession and *Question and Answer* 54 in the Heidelberg Catechism (Lord's Day XVI). In the light of the report of the synodical Gravamen Study Committee on which the synod of 1980 acted, however, this material becomes very significant. I shall therefore quote them also.

Belgic Confession, Article XVI

We believe that, all the posterity of Adam being thus fallen into perdition and ruin by the sin of our first parents, God then did manifest Himself such as He is; that is to say, merciful and just: *merciful* since He delivers and preserves from this perdition all whom He in His eternal and unchangeable counsel of mere goodness has elected in Christ Jesus our Lord, without any respect of their works; *just*, in leaving others in the fall and perdition wherein they have involved themselves.

Heidelberg Catechism
Lord's Day XXI

54. Q. What do you believe concerning the *holy catholic Church?*

A. That the Son of god, out of the whole human race, from the beginning to the end of the world, gathers, defends, and preserves for Himself, by His Spirit and Word, in the unity of the true faith, a Church chosen to everlasting life; and that I am, and forever shall remain, a living member thereof.

We shall in the ensuing pages have occasion to refer significantly to these credal statements.

In the third place, it is of the utmost importance to have before us a clear statement of what is meant by the term "reprobation," and what its place is in Dort's predestination theology. Since we should devote more attention to this than the present chapter allows, we shall in the next chapter look at what the Synod of Dort meant by God's decree of reprobation. Only by doing this will it be possible to make a fair comparison between Dort's teaching and the "elucidation" of it by the Christian Reformed Synod of 1980.

*   *   *

With the synod's acceptance of the gravamen the issue of reprobation not only came to stand squarely before the church but it invited debate and discussion by "the whole church until adjudicated."

The gravamen had been so formulated that the issue was both limited in scope and crucially fundamental in character. A gravamen against the doctrine of reprobation can follow one of three courses: argumentation based on purely scriptural data, argumentation based on doctrine, or argumentation comprising both of these courses. I chose the first course, for four reasons:

1. From boyhood at home, in school, and in the church I had been taught that God's Word written is the basis of our faith. College and seminary education strengthened this conviction with historical and theological support. I fully accepted the Reformation motto *sola Scriptura* as the norm for doctrine and life.

2. The very statements in the Canons of Dort that teach the doctrine of reprobation declare explicitly that it is "revealed in the Word of God," and that it is "the express testimony of sacred Scripture."

3. The theological argumentation in defense of reprobation is in large part rationalistic in character and speculative in no small degree, and in it the Bible plays more of a supporting than a determinative role.

4. Weightiest of all, however, was the conviction to which study over the years had brought me, namely, that there is not a shred of evidence in the entire body of Scripture for the doctrine of reprobation. If, therefore, I could show that the Bible does not teach it, there would be no need to go into the complicated reasonings and speculations of the theologians. If my analysis of Scripture was correct, and if the Christian Reformed Church lived, as she clearly claims, by the principle of *sola Scriptura*, then that would be the end of the matter.

I therefore chose a gravamen that would be based solely on scriptural data. Furthermore, this data was strictly limited to the nine passages that the Canons themselves adduced in support of its doctrine. I analyzed them in their scriptural contexts and concluded that the texts adduced are made to assume rather than establish an eternal decree of reprobation. They fall "altogether short of proving the biblical validity of the doctrine in that they do not show the existence of a divine decree which has been made in eternity which condemns a segment of mankind to eternal death . . . '' (*Acts* 1980, p. 496).

A knowledgeable friend to whom I showed my gravamen before submitting it observed, ''A good case, but they'll hang you on doctrine.'' His prophecy came true to the letter. In thus disposing of the gravamen, however, the Synod of 1980 made such concessions to my position, adopted such a novel and un-Reformed theology of reprobation, and resorted to such questionable tactics procedurally that its actions, plus those of the Synod of 1981, stand compromised biblically, theologically, and ecclesiastically. And in each case the compromise, though at times complex, is not subtle but explicit.

With this as background, we can now proceed to the matter in hand.

CHAPTER 2

WHAT IS REPROBATION?

Chapter I of the Canons of Dort sets forth the Reformed doctrines of election and reprobation. It will be helpful to see how the section is structured. It consists of eighteen *articles* of positive teaching and nine *paragraphs* of "Rejection of Errors."[1] Our concern is with the doctrine of reprobation, which is taught in Articles 6 and 15. How are these two articles related to the other sixteen?

The first five articles teach respectively that all people have sinned in Adam; that God in his love has provided a Savior from sin; that to this end the gospel is to be preached; that God's wrath rests on those who do not believe it, but those who do believe will inherit eternal life; and that the cause of unbelief and other sins is in no wise in God but in man himself, whereas faith in Christ is the free gift of God.

Having set forth these developments in salvation history, the sixth article is concerned with the eternal background of the realities of belief and unbelief in human history. Its awesome introduction to this exposition is the first sentence of the article:

> That some receive the gift of faith from God, and others do not receive it, proceeds from God's eternal decree.

This eternal decree has two sides. God "graciously softens the hearts of the elect" while "He leaves the non-elect in His just judgment to their own wickedness and obduracy." This is the "decree of election and reprobation, revealed in the Word of God," which some wrest to their own destruction, "yet to holy and pious souls affords unspeakable consolation."

With the statement of this dual decree in place, the remaining twelve articles are devoted to the exposition of election and reprobation. Articles 7–14 concern election and need not now detain us. Article 15 will engage us a great deal since it gives the full statement of Dort on the doctrine of reprobation. Article 16 is a pastoral exhortation that those who are weak in the faith, yet avail themselves of the means of grace, should not be alarmed at the mention of reprobation; on the other hand, this teaching

1. *Psalter Hymnal* section on Doctrinal Standards, pp. 44–51.

is justly terrible to unbelievers "so long as they are not seriously converted to God." Article 17 comforts godly parents with the assurance that they should not doubt the salvation of children dying in infancy; and Article 18 rebukes those who "murmur at the free grace of election and the just severity of reprobation."

This brief review of the contents of Chapter I of the Canons shows in bold relief the crucial significance of Articles 6 and 15. Their content, however brief and limited, sets forth the doctrine of reprobation in unmistakable terms. Their brevity necessarily gives the more weight to each declaration made in them. Moreover, their respective places in the structure of the chapter must be carefully noted.

Article 6 begins with a statement that briefly summarizes the whole counsel of God on the subject of predestination:

> That some receive the gift of faith from God, and others do not receive it, proceeds from God's eternal decree.

It thereupon makes a separate statement about election:

> According to which decree He graciously softens the hearts of the elect, however obstinate, and inclines them to believe;

and a separate statement about reprobation:

> while He leaves the non-elect in His just judgment to their own wickedness and obduracy.

Article 6 is then concluded as it began, namely by statements about both election and reprobation: the former is a witness to the mercy of God, the latter to the justice of God.

This is the gist of the article; however, it is necessary to point out some significant elements. According to its opening sentence, faith and unbelief are accounted for by the same decree. Both the receiving *and* the not-receiving of the gift of faith "proceed from God's eternal decree." The *one* decree works out in *two* directions. Assuming man's fallen condition, it *elects* through the softening of the hearts of the elect, and it *reprobates* by leaving the non-elect to their own wickedness. This is "that decree of election and reprobation revealed in the Word of God." What is important to notice here is that *both* election *and* reprobation are given equal decretal status. It is true, as we shall see, that Dort made a significant qualification in the Conclusion of the Canons as to the relationship of reprobation to the decree, but this in no wise compromises the eternal binding power of the decree.

Further, the fact that God "leaves" the non-elect to their own wickedness may give the impression that reprobation simply means non-election. The casual reader may be left with the thought that God overlooked the reprobate *without* having the deliberate *intention* of abandoning them to their wickedness, and therefore without taking any positive steps to effect their reprobation. Such a reading of the decree, however, Dort utterly excludes. As we shall see later, the driving power in God by which, according to Dort, he effected the reprobation of the non-elect *is the same* as that which effected the salvation of the elect. At this point we wish only to note that reprobation has a *purpose*, a rationale if you will, of the same magnitude as the purpose that underlies the decree of election. The latter is "the demonstration of His mercy" (Art. 7); the purpose of reprobation is "the declaration of his justice" (Art. 15).

These several considerations importantly raise the question: What is meant by God's "leaving" the reprobate to their wickedness, or, as Dort also calls it, his "passing by" of the reprobate? In other words, what, concretely, does "passing by" mean?

This question certainly requires an answer. Article 6 declares *that* there is a decree of reprobation, but it does not say, other than in a most general sense, *what* that declaration means. This question is answered, and answered fully, in Article 15. We must therefore take a very careful look at this article.

According to Article 15, the reprobate are those

whom God, out of His sovereign, most just, irreprehensible, and unchangeable good pleasure, has decreed

to leave in the common misery into which they have wilfully plunged themselves, and

not to bestow upon them saving faith and the grace of conversion; but, permitting them in His just judgment to follow their own ways, at last, for the declaration of His justice,

to condemn and punish them forever, not only on account of their unbelief, but also for all their other sins.

This is the core, the heart, the irreducible center and substance of the decree of reprobation. It states clearly what the "passing by" of the non-elect in fact entails. It reveals that "non-election" is not a side-effect, a by-product, or an attendant circumstance of election. Reprobation consists of three distinct decretal actions of God, deliberate, purposeful, and terribly determinative and final. The reprobate are left in a common fate of living death; they are denied the gift of faith and the grace of conversion; and they are condemned and punished forever. This does not happen simply because God elects others and in the process has a neutral attitude to those whom he "passes by." He specifically *decreed* that the reprobate should be reprobate, in the same sense in which he *decreed* that the elect should be elect. This is the meaning of the fateful words in Article 6: "That some receive the gift of faith from God, and others do not receive it, proceeds from God's eternal decree." The several parts of the decree of reprobation are therefore not due to a non-action, an omission, a disregard or inadvertence or inattention on God's part. Rather, they are the result of an explicit and purposeful decision as deliberate and intended as the decree of election.

The not-believing and the not-being-converted of the reprobate may involve all manner of time-conditioned personal circumstances, attitudes, backgrounds, and influences. The fact is that behind them and prior to them stands an immutable decree of God as unbreakable as that of election itself, determining from eternity that these circumstances, attitudes, backgrounds, and influences would never be overcome or undone by the sufficiency and power of the gospel. Before birth, from eternity, the reprobate are destined never to come to faith, are destined never to be converted, are destined to remain in the death into which their primal father Adam cast them, and are destined to be punished forever.

But this is not all. The irrevocable certainty of the fate of the damned lies in the same place, in the identical might and driving power within God that guarantees the salvation of the elect— that is, God's *sovereign good pleasure*. This is the cornerstone of God's predestinating decree, whether for election or reprobation. Not only are both achieved by the same two-sided decree, but both have their origin in the same mystery-shrouded sovereign will of God. To grasp this absolutely essential fact is to hold in hand the key to the Dortian doctrine of predestination. Let us therefore consider what this means in the present context.

In mainstream Reformed theology the decrees to elect and to reprobate are preceded by God's decree to permit Adam to fall. Both election and reprobation, therefore, have a fallen humanity as their object. For this reason the goodness or moral quality of man could form no basis at all for the election of the elect.

Therefore God elected them "out of mere grace, according to the sovereign good pleasure of His own will" (Art. 7). But it is equally true that as man's moral goodness played no role in election, so man's sin played no role in man's reprobation. The elect are elected in spite of their sin, while the reprobate are rejected not because of their sin. Both election and reprobation flow forth solely and exclusively from God's good pleasure. It is true that the elect are elected for the demonstration of God's mercy, and that the reprobate are reprobated for the demonstration of his justice. But why some are elect whereas others are reprobate is not revealed. God has so willed it. It is his "good pleasure" thus and so to dispose of the eternal fate of humans.

Now this "good pleasure" covers the entire decree of reprobation, as God in "His sovereign, most just, irreprehensible, and unchangeable good pleasure" (Art. 15) has decreed it. Therefore what God decreed was in no wise caused by the sin of the reprobate. It is the nature, the essence, the very being of the decree of God to arise solely and exclusively out of his "good pleasure."

A final but generally overlooked consideration must close this discussion of the fundamental meaning of reprobation. The same synod of Dort that brought the Canons into being also drew up a Form of Subscription that all office-bearers in the Reformed Churches of the Netherlands had to sign before taking up their ecclesiastical duties. This Form of Subscription, unchanged to this very day (with the exception of the procedure to be observed in processing a gravamen, as per the Christian Reformed Synod of 1976) must be signed by all office-bearers in the CRC, as well as by all teachers of Calvin College and Seminary. Its first paragraph states:

> We, the undersigned . . . do hereby, sincerely and in good conscience before the Lord, declare by this our subscription that we heartily believe and are persuaded that all the articles and points of doctrine contained in the Confession and Catechism of the Reformed Churches, together with the explanation of some points of the aforesaid doctrine made by the National Synod of Dordrecht, 1618-'19, do fully agree with the Word of God.

The Confession referred to in the Subscription statement is the Belgic Confession of 1563, and the "explanation of some points of the aforesaid doctrine" includes highly important references to the doctrines of election and reprobation. This is significant here in view of the manner in which the doctrines of election and reprobation are structured in Article XVI of the Confession. It reads:

> We believe that, all the posterity of Adam being thus fallen into perdition and ruin by the sin of our first parents, God then did manifest Himself such as He is; that is to say, merciful and just: **merciful**, since He delivers and preserves from this perdition all whom He in His eternal and unchangeable counsel of mere goodness has elected in Christ Jesus our Lord, without any respect to their works; **just**, in leaving others in the fall and perdition wherein they have involved themselves.

The Confession obviously teaches here that election and reprobation are joint witnesses to the essence of God's revealed being, namely that he is *merciful* and that he is *just*, the two *together* constituting the uniqueness of the divine Being. This very same dual declaration is found in Articles 6, 7, and 15 of the Canons. Article 6 has the full parallelism within itself; Articles 7 and 15 clearly show the same parallelism in their teachings on election and reprobation respectively.

The following schematizations are mine, but they are in their entire extent literal quotations from the articles in question. Read Article 6 across the page.

Article 6

Election	Common	Reprobation
That some receive the gift of faith from God		and others do not receive it,
	proceeds from God's eternal decree. According to which decree	
He graciously softens the hearts of the elect . . .		while He leaves the non-elect in His just judgment to their own wickedness and obduracy.
	And herein especially is displayed the profound,	
the merciful,	and at the same time	the righteous
	discrimination between men equally involved in ruin; or that decree of	

election	and	reprobation,
	revealed in the Word	
	of God . . .	

Article 7 defines election, and Article 15 defines reprobation. When the quoted segments are compared one by one, we find that the statements correspond to each other antithetically. The italicized words sharply set off the deliberate character of the respective antitheses.

Article 7	*Article 15*
Election	*Reprobation*
This elect number . . . God	whom [the non-elect] God . . .
has decreed	*has decreed*
to give to Christ to be	*to leave* in the common
saved by Him and	miscry into which they
	have wilfully plunged
	themselves, and
effectually *to call* and draw	
them to His communion . . .	
to bestow upon them true	*not to bestow* upon them
faith, justification, and	saving faith and the grace
sanctification; and . . .	of conversion; but . . .
finally to *glorify* them	*at last* . . . to *condemn* and
	punish them forever
for the demonstration of	*for the declaration* of
His mercy, and for the	His justice . . . .[2]
praise of . . . His glorious	
grace	

Obviously, the two decrees stand as full, irreproachable equals in the counsel of God, declaring the severity of his reprobating justice as decisively as the blessedness of his elective mercy.

This parallelism between election and reprobation in the Canons of Dort is fully carried through in the chapter titles of the official Latin, Dutch, and (Christian Reformed) English versions. The titles for Chapter I are DE DIVINA PRAEDESTINATIONE (i.e., election *and* reprobation), VAN DE GODDELIJKE VERKIEZING EN VERWERPING, and DIVINE ELECTION AND REPROBATION respectively.

In both the Belgic Confession and the Canons of Dort, therefore, the doctrine of reprobation plays a singularly important role. It constitutes, along with and co-equal to election, a testimony to the being and character of God, which are definable in terms of two attributes, mercy and justice. To the

---

2. *Condemn* and *for the declaration* of are inverted here to show the parallelism more clearly.

demonstration of these two attributes in God the whole of humanity is dedicated, in heaven and in hell, through all the unending ages of eternity. This is clear not only from the structure of the credal data, but also and most particularly from its content. Whether or not this Dortian conception is correct is not at issue here. We are only trying to understand what Dort's doctrine of reprobation basically teaches.

In view of all these considerations, the frequently raised question about the "equal ultimacy" of election and reprobation is irrelevant for anyone who takes the creeds seriously. Is God's sovereign good pleasure as expressed in the decree of reprobation less sovereign, less good, less divinely pleasurable than the same sovereign good pleasure that is expressed in election? Does reprobation proceed from God's decree with less finality, with less absoluteness, with less ultimacy than election? Is the element of justice less essential in God's being than mercy? To ask these questions is to answer them. Any attempt to minimize the finality of the reprobating side of God's dual predestination as taught by Dort and the Belgic Confession can be nothing less than a distortion of the delivered doctrine. It is possible—and indeed highly necessary—to discuss whether Dort's teaching of reprobation has any foundation at all in the Scriptures. But it is not possible with any show of theological and intellectual integrity to question that, according to Dort, reprobation is a decree of God in the same binding, irreversible, and ultimate sense that election is.

Having noted these several characteristics of the doctrine of reprobation, especially in their relationship to the doctrine of election, we must be very careful not to allow the weight or significance of reprobation to depend on considerations of balance, symmetry, emphasis, or amount of space employed in its exposition. It is not in the reciprocities of parallelism that the intrinsic issue raised by the doctrine of reprobation is found. The issue in weighing and assessing all these considerations is only and exclusively this: *Is the doctrine of reprobation true*? Does it reflect a God-ordained and God-effected *reality*? Whether with few words or many words; whether in elaborate exposition or simple statement; whether in point for point antithetic correspondence; whether as a separate decree or as a companion decree or as the negative side of one and the same decree—the central, essential issue is this: Has God from eternity destined some of humankind never, never to be able to believe the gospel? Does Scripture teach a decree "whereby a massive segment of mankind . . . is consigned to damnation before they ever come into being"? To this question Dort's answer is an unqualified Yes. To this same question the answer of the gravamen is an unqualified No.

*   *   *

With this discussion I consider that the meaning of reprobation according to the teachings of the Canons of Dort has been sufficiently set forth for the purposes of this book. Aspects of the reprobation problem raised in the synodical study committee report not dealt with in this chapter will be discussed as the need arises.

To avoid leaving the impression that I have ignored certain relevant data, I must allude to two matters that are frequently adduced to justify the downplaying of reprobation. One is the rejection in the Conclusion of the Canons of the teaching imputed to them that "in the same manner in which election is the fountain and cause of faith and good works, reprobation is the cause of unbelief and impiety"; the other is the alleged support for the mitigation of reprobation found in the theological teaching of infralapsarianism. Since neither the rejection of the former nor the acceptance of the latter deprives Dortian reprobation of its finality, I shall not detain the reader at this point with these fundamentally irrelevant matters. Instead I shall comment briefly on both in an appendix.

CHAPTER 3

THEOLOGY BY COMMITTEE

The gravamen that I submitted to the Synod of 1977 was directed against the doctrine of reprobation as it is taught in the Canons of Dort, Chapter I, Articles 6 and 15. What this teaching contains, as the gravamen understands it, has been set forth in the preceding chapter. The gravamen examined all the Scripture passages to which the Canons refer in their declaration of the doctrine. I expected that if my exegesis[1] were found to be correct, the incriminated doctrine would be abandoned as an official teaching of the Christian Reformed Church.

The study committee appointed by the Synod of 1977 was charged "to study the gravamen in the light of Scripture, and to advise the Synod of 1980 as to the cogency of the gravamen and how it should further be dealt with by synod" (*Acts*, p. 486).

In the course of its work the committee, with minor reservations, found my exegesis altogether correct. It agreed that such passages as "who works all things after the counsel of his will" (Eph. 1:11); "is it not lawful for me to do what I will with my own" (Matt. 20:15); "he has mercy on whom he will and whom he wills he hardens" (Rom. 9:18); "Jacob I loved but Esau I hated" (Rom. 9:13) had been wrongly understood by the church.

The Synod of 1980, in approving the committee's findings and recommending them to the church as an "elucidation" of the teachings of the Canons on election and reprobation, thereby in one sweeping action (reinforced by the Synod of 1981) removed the entire scriptural basis that has historically undergirded the doctrine of reprobation as understood in the Reformed churches.

By no means, however, did the study committee report agree that the Reformed doctrine of reprobation as taught by Dort had been invalidated by the new interpretation of textual material. While agreeing that my exegesis was faithful to Scripture, it held—emphatically—that my exegesis was "irrelevant." Its irrelevance arose from the alleged fact that the gravamen had wholly misread

---

1. A technical theological word meaning "explanation or analytical interpretation of a text."

the Canons on the subject of reprobation. The Canons do not teach what the gravamen alleges them to teach. Therefore its exegesis, while wholly correct in itself, is also wholly beside the point.

From the gravamen point of view, it is no small gain that the scriptural basis that has supported the doctrine of reprobation for three and a half centuries no longer exists. At the same time, however, the committee report holds that Dort's doctrine of reprobation is deeply rooted in Scripture. This raises the intriguing question of how the committee understands the scriptural character of Dort's doctrine. This important matter will be taken up in due course.

At this point I shall quote three consecutive paragraphs in the study committee's report on which its entire case against the gravamen rests:

Clearly one focus of Boer's objection to what he takes to be the teaching of the Canons on reprobation is their teaching, on his interpretation, that God is the cause of unbelief. For example, on p. 339 of the gravamen he says, "The statement in the Canons, 'That some receive the gift of faith from God and others do not receive it, proceeds from God's eternal decree (Chap. I, Art. 6),' is in its second part untrue and constitutes a denial of the nondisclosure in the Word of God of any cause of unbelief other than the heart of man." And again, on page 335, "All who wish to find backgrounds, occasion, or explanation for unbelief in any other area than that of human responsibility within the dimension of history will forever have their way barred by Jesus' lament over Jerusalem. . . ." And again, on page 338, ". . . there is no eternal decree that withholds repentance and faith from anyone. Unbelief is from the beginning to the end of Scripture the fault and responsibility of man himself."

A second focus of Boer's objection is the teaching of the Canons, as he interprets them, that certain human beings are consigned to damnation before they ever exist, and thus apart from any merit or demerit on their part. For example, on page 340 of the gravamen he speaks of human beings as being, in the Canons' teaching, "consigned to everlasting damnation before they ever came into being." And on page 341, in his summation, he speaks of "a sovereign wrath that damns men to an existence of everlasting death without regard to any demerit on their part."

It seems clear that it is especially on these two matters that the issue is joined between Boer, on the one hand, and the Canons as he reads them on the other: that an eternal decree of God is the cause of unbelief, and that human beings are consigned to damnation before they ever exist and apart from anything that they actually do.[2]

The second of the three paragraphs quoted above I acknowledge as a fair statement of my position. I have, however, a reservation about the first paragraph. I am not aware that in my gravamen I charge Dort in so many words with making God the cause of unbelief. I say that we are not allowed to seek backgrounds, occasion, or explanation of unbelief in any area beyond the dimension of human history; that to do so is to deny the non-disclosure of such backgrounds in God's Word; and that there is no decree that withholds repentance and faith from anyone. That Dort affirms these things seems to me to be beyond doubt, and that it thereby involves God in the cause of unbelief seems also beyond doubt. But I would have the carefulness and circumspection with which I attributed these things to Dort recognized by the critical reader. I consider it all the more appropriate to say this in view of Dort's repeated declarations that God is *not* the cause of sin and unbelief, in I/5 stating specifically that the "cause or guilt of this unbelief . . . is *no wise* in God." I consider Dort to be involved in a profound self-contradiction here rather than being guilty of a direct teaching that God is the cause of unbelief.

With all this in mind, we come now to the important matter of setting forth the study committee's exposition of what reprobation is *according to the teaching of Dort*. This is important not only because of its own theological content but also and not least because this now constitutes the official Christian Reformed Church understanding of reprobation.

As we examine it, we must constantly keep before us the fundamental difference between the position of the gravamen and that of the study committee report. The issue presented by the three paragraphs from the report quoted above can be reduced to one simple question. It is:

2. *Acts of Synod*, 1980, p. 529. Unless otherwise indicated, further page references refer to the same source. The text of the gravamen can be found in the *Acts of Synod*, 1977. The report of the study committee can also be found in the *Agenda* of 1980. Quotations in this book taken from the committee's report can be located in the *Agenda* of 1980 by subtracting 157 from the page references to the *Acts*. The committee's references to the gravamen are found in the *Agenda* of 1980.

Does or does not the reprobation of men attributed to God by the Canons of Dort bring into being a segment of humankind which, because of God's eternal decree, can never under any circumstances come to salvation?

That is the critical issue, and basically there is no other issue. The synods of 1980 and 1981, the study committee, and I are all agreed that the Bible passages traditionally adduced as evidence for the doctrine of reprobation *do not teach it*. Since the study committee and two synods nevertheless hold that the Bible *does* teach reprobation, the question we face is: What is this new position, what is the basis for it, and is it valid?

* * *

The Synod of 1980 officially rejected the gravamen against the doctrine of reprobation in the following decision that constitutes a verbatim adoption of the recommendation of the gravamen study committee:

> That synod do not accede to the request made in Dr. Harry Boer's Confessional-Revision Gravamen: namely, that "the doctrine of reprobation ought . . . to be exscinded from or become a nonbinding part of the creeds of the Christian Reformed Church" (Gravamen, p. 330).
>
> *Grounds:*
> a. The Canons of Dort do not teach what the gravamen erroneously understands the doctrine of reprobation to be: namely, a decree by means of which God is the cause of man's unbelief, and by means of which God has from eternity consigned certain human beings to damnation apart from any merit or demerit on their part.
> b. The Scriptures do teach a doctrine of election and reprobation in that they teach that some but not all have been elected to eternal life. (p. 76)

This altogether remarkable decision, carefully crafted in every respect, summarizes completely the thrust and intent of the study committee report.

One asks, where in this understanding of Dort's teaching do we find the doctrine of reprobation? It is found in ground **b**. There reprobation is spoken of in these words: "not all have been elected to eternal life." Reprobation then would seem to be not-having-been-elected. But how can this be a statement of what reprobation is? To say that a horse is not a cow, or that a tree is not a rock is true enough, but it hardly tells us what a horse is or what a tree is.

What, then, is the present understanding of the Christian Reformed Church's confession with respect to reprobation? The remainder of this chapter is concerned to answer that question.

1. IS "PASSING BY" A FACET OF ELECTION?

There is no heretical idea so indignantly rejected in the Canons of Dort as the thought that God is the cause or author of sin and unbelief. I have earlier in this chapter indicated that these protestations are to be taken seriously and that, consequently, I have not in wholly unreserved language accused Dort of teaching this. We are all aware, however, that in judging large and complex affairs it is most unwise to be guided by simple affirmations or denials, however honestly and sincerely these may be made, while remaining blind to the essential nature and structure of a matter.

We are faced with the declaration of Article 6, "That some receive the gift of faith from God, and others do not receive it, proceeds from God's eternal decree." It is clear, therefore, that *before* God created the world a relationship was established between God's decree and man's believing or not believing the gospel. However we may understand the relationship of eternity to time (more on this later), there can be no doubt about the fact that, so far as Dort's thinking is concerned, what God decreed in eternity was determinative of what would eventuate in time. This is clear in the case of election, ". . . as He has chosen His own from eternity in Christ, so He calls them effectually in time . . ." (III-IV/10). Since reprobation belongs to the same decree as election (I/6), this would also apply to it.

If, therefore, God's decree determines in eternity that a certain segment of humanity shall be left in their sin and thereby passed by for salvation, if that same decree determines that they shall not receive the gift of faith and the grace of conversion, if it further decrees that they shall be condemned and punished forever for sins done in time, and if this is all effectuated in time and according to God's sovereign good pleasure, then it would appear that God is inextricably involved in the sin and unbelief of those so reprobated and that there is no way in which the reprobate could have escaped this fate. When the reprobate are born they are by the fact of birth introduced into a state of lostness from which it is not possible for them ever to extricate themselves, or from which any other can extricate them. They are the objects of an unbreakable, irreversible, eternal divine decree through which they are destined forever to be a witness to the justice of God.

Moreover, the concept of God's "good pleasure" must at this point be taken with full seriousness. It means that God, whether in electing or in reprobating, was not guided, conditioned, or influenced in the slightest degree by any quality, whether good or bad, *either* in the elect *or* in the reprobate. God's "good pleasure" means simply what it says, namely that God was pleased to act thus or so for reasons that are wholly unknown and closed to us. We can say *that* God elected and reprobated; we cannot say *why* he elected and reprobated, other than that he *was pleased* so to act. The study committee emphasizes this with special reference to God's reprobating decree: "In harmony with the teaching of I/6 and I/15 . . . the committee affirms that no other cause can be found for the *passing by* than God's sovereign good pleasure" (p. 517).

In short, the reprobate are passed by for salvation *without regard to any condition of sin, unbelief, or other factors* disqualifying them from being recipients of the saving grace of God.

The study committee resolutely refuses to face the significance of these hard facts, textured into the very warp and woof of the decretal fabric. Indeed, it exerts itself to remove this significance. The controlling impression left by its report is that of a contentless "passing over" of non-elect in eternity that seems to sustain no meaningful or distinguishable relationship to the unbelief of the reprobate or to the judgment on them at the end of time. Consider the following quotations from the report:

> The fact that I/15 speaks of "the decree of reprobation" should not be understood as implying that this is a separate decree or decision of God which stands wholly by itself, independent of the decree of election. The decree or decision of reprobation is to be thought of as an aspect of a single decree or decision. The fact that I/6 speaks of a "decree of election and reprobation" makes this clear, as does also the statement in I/8, "There are not various decrees of election, but one and the same decree. . . ." It should be noted in addition that even I/15, which speaks of "the decree of reprobation," begins with a discussion of election, going on to say that it is the testimony

of Scripture that "not all, but some only, are elected, while others are passed by. . . . " In other words, that Canons in I/15 understand God's passing by of some not as the content of a separate decree but as an action of God which is involved in, and therefore a facet of, the one decree of election. (p. 517)

. . . God consigns someone to destruction only on the basis of what that person does. . . . (p. 521)

Damnation is a response to the evil the "reprobates" do, of which God is not the cause. . . . (p. 522)

Reprobation enters the Canons only insofar as is necessary to secure the Reformed doctrine of particular or individual election. . . . (p. 522)

They [the Contra-Remonstrants at the Conference in the Hague] considered reprobation implicit in the biblical teaching of election. . . . (p. 523)

It is important for understanding the structure of Dort's thinking that "reprobation" understood as passing over (*preterition*) be clearly distinguished from the decree of *condemnation*. (p. 519)

What the Canons teach, so far as condemnation is concerned (and I/15 understands reprobation as including the decree of condemnation) is that God condemns to destruction only those who do, in fact, sin and exhibit unbelief. . . . Human beings are condemned only on the basis of what they actually do in history. (p. 530)

For Calvin, implicit in the biblical teaching about the setting apart or electing of some to salvation is the passing by of others. (p. 524)

Does Dort teach that before the existence of human beings, thus before they have done anything, God consigns some to destruction wholly apart from what they may do? . . . the answer is most emphatically, "No." (p. 521)

Dort's thought is clearly that if those who are passed over for faith, and thus ultimately condemned, *had* performed all the works of righteousness, they would receive salvation. (p. 521)

The *Conclusion* rejects the charge that the Reformed churches teach that "God, by a mere arbitrary act of his will, without the least respect or view to any sin, has predestinated the greatest part of the world to eternal damnation, and has created them for this very purpose. . . . " (p. 521)

The theme that runs through, and gives a basic unity to, all these quotations is that there are not really two decrees affecting the eternal fate of humankind. There is only one decree, the decree of election. In this election God "passed over" those who were not elected. The meaning of this "passing over" as set forth in Article 15 receives little attention at the committee's hand. It is an "aspect" of election; it is an action of God that is "involved in" and therefore a "facet" of what the committee calls "the one decree of election." What Article 6 plainly calls "that decree of election and reprobation" now becomes "that decree of election," which has a certain negative "aspect" or "facet" associated with it. In the Canons this aspect or facet has somehow or other been dignified with the word "decree." Condemnation or damnation is severed from the decretal root and now becomes simply a divine "response to the evil that the reprobate do," a statement with which no Arminian would disagree. Reprobation has no purpose distinctive to itself. Its decretally assigned function of demonstrating the stern face of God's justice suddenly becomes inoperative—so much so, in fact, that this (in Dort's judgment) highly important side of the decree receives no more than a passing glance in the committee report. *God's being* (Belgic Confession, Art. XVI) plays no role in the new look of 1980 in its assessment of the significance of reprobation in the Canons of Dort.

We should also not overlook what the committee does with quotation marks to demote the doctrine of reprobation from the credal status accorded it by Dort. Section V of the committee's report is concerned with the continued functioning of the Canons in the church. Part 3 of that Section is entitled: Can "Reprobation" be Preached? Part 4 is entitled: Is the "Doctrine of Reprobation" a Hindrance to Preaching? (p. 555). There is no good reason why in Reformed theology reprobation and doctrine of reprobation should be enclosed in quotation marks. The doctrine is an integral part of the tradition. The committee's use of quotation marks indicates a skeptical or condescending if not a rejecting attitude to the quoted matter. This impression is strengthened when in Parts 5 and 6 the headings read straightforwardly: Is the Doctrine of Election a Hindrance to Preaching? and: How Should the Doctrine of Election be Preached? (p. 557). Given its view of "reprobation," the committee has very good reason indeed to use quotation marks as it does. The question is: Is this an "elucidation" or an obscuration of the Canons? For the reader should mind well that the committee rejected the gravamen not on basis of its own insights into the doctrine of reprobation, but on basis of *what Dort teaches about reprobation*.

So eager was the committee to reinforce its downgrading of reprobation that it ignored its own more correct translation of

I/15 in favor of the quite incorrect translation of a particular passage in the version found in the *Psalter Hymnal*. As noted before, Article 15 is devoted in its entirety to the exposition of the doctrine of reprobation. The committee, reluctant to grant this, states that it begins "with a discussion of election," and it quotes from the article as follows: "not all, but some only, are elected while others are passed by . . . ." The correct translation, the committee's own (p. 514), is "that not all men have been chosen, but that some have not been chosen or have been passed by . . . ." Far from "discussing" election, these words reinforce by a triple negation the doctrine of reprobation.

Moved by the same concern, the committee put into the mouth of Dort a position that no theologian there present would appropriate as his own. Dort is presented as teaching "clearly" that "if the reprobate had performed all the works of righteousness they would receive salvation." Dort did nothing of the kind. In its well-known Conclusion it admonished the faithful to pay no heed to calumnies heaped on the faith of the Reformed Churches from every side or to private expressions of some, often dishonestly quoted or corrupted and wrested to another than their intended meaning. Among these was the charge that "if the reprobate should even perform truly all the works of the saints, their obedience would not in the least contribute to their salvation." This charge the synod rejected. It made no statement as to how it could in some way have a legitimate place in Reformed theology. But that is what the committee makes of it, and not merely in some small way, but as it stands in its report. In the context of Dort's teaching of election and reprobation the charge is obviously absurd. A reprobate is one who by definition is dead in sins and trespasses, incapable of any good work, left to his own wickedness, denied faith and conversion, and condemned to eternal punishment—and all this as an outflow and realization in life of a decree of God's good pleasure.

What we have done so far in this chapter is to illustrate the committee's pervasive devaluation of reprobation in the Canons. The apparent point to which this process inevitably drives the church is to hold to "passing over" as an in effect meaningless phrase. Meanwhile, continuous and detailed emphasis on condemnation as purely time conditioned and therefore without relationship to an eternal decree removes all distinction between the Dortian and the Arminian conceptions of the divine judgment. This comes starkly to the fore in two of the cited quotations:

> It is important for understanding the structure of Dort's thinking that "reprobation" understood as passing over (*preterition*) be clearly distinguished from the decree of *condemnation*. (p. 519)

> . . . God condemns to destruction only those who do, in fact, sin and exhibit unbelief, and that he does so only *on the basis of* their sin and unbelief. Human beings are condemned only on the basis of what they actually do in history. (p. 530)

There are two extremely disturbing factors here. The first is the disjunction between passing over and condemnation, and the second is the complete obscuration of the significance of passing over in the statement defining condemnation. The latter especially is deceptive because, as it stands, the statement is correct. No one can argue with it in isolation from its context. The problem of reprobation does not confront us with any difficulties on the score of the relationship of judgment to sin. The problem of reprobation is this: Since the reprobate have by Adam's disobedience fallen into sin, and since God has decreed (1) to leave them in their wickedness and obduracy, (2) not to grant them the gift of faith and the grace of conversion, and (3) to condemn and punish them forever, do they have a true and genuine opportunity to believe the gospel and be saved? That is the sole and exclusive problem of reprobation in Reformed theology. Dort's answer to that question is obviously No. If, however, it is said to be Yes, how must we construe God's eternal decree to have been annulled? In short, with what right does the study committee judge God's passing over of the reprobate to be a sort of by-product, a facet, an aspect of election, something which is "involved in" election, but which does not decisively affect their lives? The finally determinative factor in their lives, says the committee report, is "what they actually do in history." Have the church and her theologians over the years and through the centuries made a decretal mountain out of a by-product mole-hill? Did Calvin have a "facet" of election in mind when he referred to reprobation as a *decretum horribile*?[3] Did Abraham Kuyper have an "aspect" of election in mind when

---

3. *Institutes of the Christian Religion*, Book III, Chap. 23, Par. 7. Calvin writes: "The decree, I admit, is dreadful; and yet it is impossible to deny that God foreknew what the end of man was to be before he made him, and foreknew, because he had so ordained by his decree."

he spoke of the decree of reprobation as *"gruwelijk"* (gruesome)?
Is it to be received as a valid interpretation of Dort that the final
judgment that condemns the reprobate to eternal perdition bears
no discernible relationship to the decree to pass by the non-elect?
What is the function of the passing by if not to bring into being
those who shall be condemned to demonstrate the glory of God's
justice? We shall consider this question in greater detail in the
following section.

2. THE UNPARDONABLE OMISSION

The basic statement of the separation between "passing by" and
"condemnation" in the committee report is as follows:

> In I/6 the phrase "that decree of election and reprobation" . . . refers
> to reprobation in its narrower sense, as the equivalent of nonelection
> or passing by, with only God's good pleasure as its cause. In I/15,
> however, the phrase "and this is the decree of reprobation" . . . refers
> to reprobation in its broader sense, as embracing both preterition
> (nonelection, or passing by) with God's good pleasure as its cause,
> and damnation, with man's sin as its cause.
>
> In this report, whenever there is a danger of being misunderstood,
> we shall make clear in which sense we are using the word *reproba-
> tion*. In harmony with the teaching of I/6 and I/15, however, the
> committee affirms that no other cause can be found for the *passing
> by* than God's sovereign good pleasure, whereas the cause of *con-
> demnation* is man's sin and unbelief. (pp. 516–17)

This disjunction between passing by and condemnation inevitably
raises the question whether, after all, a way of salvation remains
open to the reprobate. The crucial point of debate in the reprobation question is not whether unbelievers are punished for sins
committed in the course of their lives, but whether or not a divine
decree forever bars them from the possibility of faith. Does
condemnation follow inevitably upon God's passing them by for
salvation, or does it not? This question, this inevitable question,
the committee does not face.

The committee might challenge this criticism by calling attention to the following passage in its report:

> A question that you and I might be inclined to ask, again, is, *When*
> did God decide to pass over certain persons with respect to the gift
> of faith, with the consequence that they are consigned to the destruc-
> tion of which their sin has made them worthy? Did he make this

decision before they ever sinned—indeed, before they ever existed? And again, the answer that Dort might very well have given is that this is an inappropriate question. There is no "when" to the eternal decrees of the eternal God. God did not make this decision before they ever existed or sinned. But neither did he make it after they existed or sinned. (p. 519)

Of immediate relevance here is the statement used in connection with God's passing over of the reprobate: "with the consequence that they are consigned to the destruction of which their sin has made them worthy." Taken by themselves, these words mean that condemnation is an inevitable outcome of the passing over, in which case there would be no question of disjunction. But this clear meaning of the words in and of themselves is immediately cast into question by the "when" of the passing over. How can the passing over have the "consequence" of destruction when there is the greatest kind of ambiguity with respect to its relationship to the existence and sin of the reprobate? When one adds to this the unrelieved emphasis on unbelief and sin *in history* as the sole cause of the condemnation of the reprobate, it is hardly reasonable to give face value to one highly equivocal reference pointing in a different direction.

Moreover, there are other questions that only deepen the ambiguity that we face in this connection. If God did not decree to pass the reprobate by *before* they ever existed or sinned, and if he did not decree to pass them by *after* they existed or sinned, one cannot but wonder whether he passed them by at all. To this rather reasonable reaction our committee does not address itself. The ambiguity posed by its neither-nor position at this point is heightened by the observation that Dort "might well have given" the answer that the whole "when" question is out of order. I submit that in this crucial matter we are little helped by speculations about what Dort "might well" have said in relation to the committee's uncertainties. Dort has spoken very clearly and the issue is whether, having spoken as it did, it has spoken scripturally.

These observations about the disjunction between passing over and condemnation raise a fundamental issue with respect to the study committee's report. At issue is its failure to deal with the *massive unity* of the doctrine of reprobation as it is set forth in I/15. One would have expected the committee, seeing its basic argument, to take serious note of this. Such an expectation was warranted, if only by its own words at the beginning of its exposition of the doctrine. Under the heading D. *Analysis of the Canons, with Specific Reference to Their Teaching on Reprobation* (p. 517), the committee writes:

> In connection with our mandate, the committee conducted an in-depth study of the Canons of Dort, to see whether they do indeed teach what the gravamen claims they teach. What follows next, therefore, is an analysis of the Canons focused on what they say concerning reprobation.

A true in-depth study of the kind the committee undertook could not, in my judgment, fail to take the most serious note of the *structure*, particularly the *grammatical* structure, of the doctrine of reprobation as set forth in I/15. Nowhere in Reformed theology has grammar ever been used more advisedly to articulate a theological conception than in the Dortian exposition of its doctrine of reprobation.

The committee has made very plain that reprobation in the sense of passing by is an aspect, a facet, or to put it more colloquially, a spin-off of the decree of election. In a sort of grudging way it is willing to call this passing by a decree, but obviously it does not have the status of the decree of election. Nevertheless, insofar as one can speak of reprobation as a decree, God's passing by or passing over constitutes this decree "in its narrower sense." But the committee also speaks of reprobation "in its broader sense," which includes both passing by and condemnation.

In no sense is this the language of Dort. Article 15 states:

> that not all men have been chosen, but that some have not been chosen or have been passed by in God's eternal election

and *then* follows the declaration that sets forth what these three synonymous statements *mean*. This declaration states what reprobation *in fact is*. With respect to those who "have been passed by" in God's eternal election, Dort declares:

> . . . whom God, out of his sovereign, most just, irreprehensible, and unchangeable good pleasure, *has decreed*
> 1. *to leave in the common misery* into which they have wilfully plunged themselves, and
> 2. *not to bestow upon them saving faith and the* grace of conversion; but, permitting them in his just judgment to follow their own ways, at last, for the declaration of his justice,
> 3. *to condem and punish them forever*, not only on account of their unbelief, but also for all their other sins.

The committee's own translation, in general a commendable improvement on the Christian Reformed English version, at this point becomes regrettably capricious. Both the official Latin and the official Dutch versions present the following order of thought:

> . . . whom God out of his sovereign, most just, irreprehensible and unchangeable good pleasure has decreed: 1) to leave . . . and 2) not to bestow . . . but . . . 3) to condemn and punish forever . . . .

The committee's translation reads:

> . . . concerning whom God has made the following decision: 1) to leave them, out of his entirely free, most just, irreproachable, and unchangeable good pleasure, in the common misery . . . 2) not to endow them . . . but at long last 3) to condemn and eternally punish . . . .

This wholly abritrary order makes the crucially important "good pleasure" apply only to the first of the three phases of reprobation. This may seem to support the disjunction between passing by and condemnation, but it is at the expense of grammatical and theological integrity. Dort just didn't propound her theology in this way. Neither the official Latin nor the official Dutch word order permits this awkward and misleading limitation of God's good pleasure.

Let us, then, look at the statement more closely. The subject is "God." The verb is "decreed." The object of the verb, that is, the object of God's decreeing action, consists of three verbal forms beginning with "to": "to leave," "to-not-bestow," and "to condemn and punish." These verbal forms, in turn, have a common object, namely "whom," that is, the reprobate. This is all plain enough and the reader can flesh out the skeleton for himself or herself.

There is, however, a sleeper in the picture that is easy to overlook. It consists of the words that articulate *how*, in what *manner*, God "decreed." God's decree was made in accordance with his "good pleasure." This good pleasure is sovereign, most just, irreprehensible, and unchangeable. Most important of all is to note that this "good pleasure," so described, applies to *all* three of God's decreeing utterances. According to his *good pleasure* he decreed:

1. to leave the reprobate in the common misery
2. to-not-bestow on them saving faith and the grace of conversion
3. to condemn and punish them forever.

These are the grammatical facts that determine the theological relationships of the data. Their significance in the present instance is far-reaching indeed.

Dort teaches that God decreed reprobation. This, however, is only half of the decretal action. God decreed reprobation *in a certain way*. He decreed the threefold content, above noted, of the reprobates' doom according to his sovereign, most just, irreprehensible, and unchangeable *good pleasure*. This good pleasure, in every way omnipotent and faultless, was the sphere, the disposition, within which God ordained the bliss of the elect and the fate of the reprobate. This determinative circumstance gives a cast to the decree of reprobation that is of the utmost significance for the understanding of reprobation in its deepest meaning. We are fortunate that whatever serious differences may obtain between the committee's and the gravamen's diverse understandings of Dort, there is one crucial theological point on the meaning of which they are quite agreed, namely their common understanding of what is meant by "God's good pleasure" in the Canons of Dort and in Reformed theology in general. Both see it as a sort of theological code expression for the unrevealed cause of a given divine action. In the case of reprobation the cause is sovereign, most just, irreprehensible, and unchangeable, but the nature of the divine action so described is not made known. God was "pleased" so to act. Beyond this we dare not speak. With respect to both election and reprobation, however, Reformed theology, in view of its confrontations with Arminianism, uniformly and specifically *excludes* a humanly conceivable cause for God's decree. This is to say that there is nothing in man, in his being, his good or his evil, that constrained God to elect some and to reprobate others. Thus the committee affirms that "in harmony with the teaching of I/6 and I/15 . . . . no other cause can be found for the *passing by* than God's sovereign good pleasure."

When we consider what this means in the context of the present discussion, we note first of all that God decreed *in his good pleasure* three distinct judgments on the reprobate: *to leave* them in the common misery; *to withhold* from them the gift of faith and the grace of conversion; and *to condemn* and punish them forever. This calls into question a central thesis in the study committee's exposition of the teaching of Dort. It holds that while the passing by for salvation is caused solely by God's sovereign good pleasure, "the cause of condemnation is man's sin and unbelief." In their words, "God consigns someone to destruction only on the basis of what that person does . . . " (p. 521). And again, the committee reports the Canons as teaching "that God condemns to destruction only those who do, in fact, sin and exhibit unbelief . . . . Human beings are condemned only on the basis of what they actually do in history" (p. 530).

How can this be squared with the clear declaration of Dort that the reprobate are condemned and punished for their sins according to God's good pleasure?

Without regard to unbelief, sin, failure, or demerit of any kind, God ordained that some human beings should remain in the sin into which they had plunged themselves. Without regard to unbelief, sin, failure, or demerit of any kind, God ordained "not to bestow" on those same human beings the gift of faith and the grace of conversion.

The unavoidable question is, therefore, whether there is any conceivable possibility that human beings destined for such irreversible subjection to sin and unbelief, and thus utterly denied faith and conversion, should escape condemnation and punishment? Is not the third member of the triad of judgments pronounced over the reprobate wholly in harmony with and complementary to the first two?

It is because of this question that I have pressed and emphasized the disjunction that the committee makes between passing over and condemnation. The committee report has not a word to say about the relationship between the triad of judgments pronounced over the reprobate and the sovereign good pleasure of God that effects these judgments. The committee speaks only and exclusively about God's passing over of the non-elect that flows from his good pleasure, and the condemnation of the reprobate that is exclusively based on their unbelief and sin. What about his decree to leave the reprobate in the common misery into which they have plunged themselves? Are they able to be extricated from it? The answer obviously is No. What about the decree withholding from them the gift of faith and the grace of conversion? Can the reprobate somehow obtain this faith and this conversion? Again the answer obviously is No.

Do these two No's not make their condemnation and punishment inevitable? Are all three judgments not indivisible parts of one unalterable decree? What, then, is the point of the committee report in constantly and repeatedly and insistently saying that the sole cause of their condemnation and punishment is their sin done in history? One is left with the distinct impression that their being reprobated to be left in the common misery and their being denied the grace of salvation have nothing at all to do with their fate to be condemned and punished forever. The reprobate would seem to begin life with a perfectly blank page, and only what history writes on that page will be the basis for their condemnation and punishment. Failure to relate the sovereign good pleasure of God's decree to its triad of judgments on the reprobate is the unpardonable omission in the gravamen study committee report.

Even so, we must deal with the quite reasonable question: How can God's decree to condemn and punish the reprobate be said to be made in his "good pleasure," when in fact he condemns and punishes them "not only on account of their unbelief but also for all their other sins"?

The problem will be simplified if we compare it to a similar situation in the case of election. Every elect person is born in a state of election. In the course of God's providence he discovers the elect state to which he has been ordained. He lives the life of faith and obedience, and at its end will receive from God a reward of grace. This reward is according to his works and the measure of his faith, and this will vary from elect person to elect person. No one would say, however, that his good works and his faith are *the cause* of his reward. The cause of the reward is exclusively God's sovereign good pleasure in which the worth and merit of the individual played no role. The rewards of the righteous are in very truth rewards *of grace*. God is pleased, however, to apportion reward *according to the measure* of the believer's faith and obedience.

The parallelism of the structures in which Dort sets forth the doctrines of election and reprobation apply here also—and, it may be added, not least here. The reprobate are reprobate from eternity and as reprobate they stand condemned from eternity. The *extent* or *measure* of the punishment that they will receive, however, will be determined by the degree of their disobedience. But this may in no wise be permitted to obscure the fact that the certainty or inevitability of condemnation and punishment as such have been determined in the reprobation decree of God's good pleasure. In the court of God's decree the reprobate are declared *guilty* from eternity, but the *sentence* that is pronounced upon them is determined by their life in time.

Also in the matter of rewards and punishments, God, as Dort understood him, manifests himself such as he is, namely *merciful* and *just*.

*   *   *

In sum, the relationship that the committee establishes between God's sovereign good pleasure (i.e., God's action relative to man's perdition without reference to merit or demerit) and reprobation is solely at the point of passing by. But that is not where Dort relates God's good pleasure to the decree of reprobation. Dort relates it to the triad of judgments consisting of God's leaving the reprobate in the common misery into which they have plunged themselves, to his withholding from them the gift of faith and the grace of conversion, and to his condemning and punishing them forever. The committee report does not relate God's good pleasure to either of the first two judgments, and it affirms that man's unbelief and sin are the sole ground or cause of the condemnation of the reprobate in the third judgment. In so doing it ignores the first two elements of Dort's decree of reprobation, thoroughly misconstrues the third, and completely misrepresents the decree of reprobation as a whole.

In order to make its characteristic and determinative distinction between passing by and condemnation, it literally "passed over" the whole decree as a matter of irrelevance. That is the price the committee paid to downgrade the decree of reprobation to be an aspect and a facet of the decree of election. This incredible omission must be counted as a fatal flaw in its novel and forced interpretation of the Canons on the subject of reprobation.

It is rather interesting to observe that the committee report takes no note of the absence of an element in the gravamen around which so much of its argumentation revolves. In citing those data in Articles 6 and 15 to which the gravamen takes exception, I did not include the passage "to condemn and punish them forever, not only on account of their unbelief but also for all their other sins" (p. 487). I left this out because it invites the kind of misunderstanding the committee fell prey to, and would have lengthened an already lengthy gravamen. It was fully sufficient for the purpose of the gravamen to rest its case on the first two declarations of the decree, namely that God out of his sovereign, most just, irreprehensible, and unchangeable good pleasure *has decreed*:

> to leave [the reprobate] in the common misery into which they had wilfully plunged themselves, and
>
> not to bestow on them saving faith and the grace of conversion.

No one living under this divine unalterable determination, made without reference to merit or demerit, can ever become the recipient of the life and grace that is in Christ Jesus.

The committee itself acknowledges this fact. At the close of its theological argument, after it has recommended that the gravamen be rejected, the study committee report makes an inexplicable, surprising statement: "In recommending this disposition of the gravamen we do not wish to be taken as suggesting that the Canons are in every way satisfactory" (p. 533). Then follow a number of trenchant strictures on the Canons (which we shall note in due course), of which one is altogether pertinently relevant to the present discussion. The committee opines:

> Furthermore, it would seem to be an implication of the teachings of the Canons on reprobation, plus their teaching on the nature of our fallen condition, that for a person who never comes to faith, it was in fact always impossible that he would. (p. 533)

But is not this conceding all that the gravamen was about? Does this not mean that according to Dort there *is* a "cause of unbelief other than the heart of man"? Does this statement not propose what the committee has so thoroughly rejected, namely that there *are* "backgrounds, occasion, or explanation for unbelief" in other areas "than that of human responsibility within the dimension of history"? Can this mean other than that there *is* an "eternal decree that withholds repentance and faith" from people? Is it not true that, according to Dort, certain human beings *are* "consigned to damnation before they ever exist, and thus apart from any merit or demerit on their part"? Does not reprobation according to God's good pleasure mean *precisely* that humans are damned to "an existence of everlasting death without regard to any demerit on their part"? *Is not that exactly what reprobation is*? (All gravamen quotations from p. 529 of the committee report.)

A necessary postscript to the above paragraph is that the committee envelops eternal reprobation as taught in the Canons of Dort, Articles 6 and 15, in murky clouds of "seeming" and "implication." I submit that there is nothing tentative, provisional, vague, or uncertain in Dort's exposition of our Reformed Achilles' heel.

3. WHAT IS MEANT BY GOD'S "ETERNAL" DECREE?

The study committee takes strong exception to the statements in the gravamen that in reprobation human beings are "consigned to everlasting damnation before they ever came into being" (p. 529), and that a "sovereign wrath . . . damns men to an existence of everlasting death without regard to any demerit" (p. 529). The committee sees the *when* of reprobation (and of election) quite differently:

> And if it be asked when God made this selection, *before* they fell or *after* they fell, there is some evidence for the conclusion that for the writers of Dort the "When?" question does not apply. The decree in question is an *eternal* decree of God. What takes place in eternity, they would appear to say, does not stand in some before-and-after relation to what takes place in history. (p. 518)

And

> A question that you and I might be inclined to ask, again, is, *When* did God decide to pass over certain persons with respect to the gift of faith, with the consequence that they are consigned to the destruction of which their sin has made them worthy? Did he make this decision before they ever sinned—indeed, before they ever existed? And again, the answer that Dort might very well have given is that this is an inappropriate question. There is no "when" to the eternal decrees of the eternal God. God did not make this decision before they ever existed or sinned. But neither did he make it after they existed or sinned. (p. 519)

The problem that arises here is that of the relationship of time to eternity. That there is mystery here is beyond doubt. In all considerations of eternity we are dealing with a reality that can be neither experienced nor defined while yet our time-conditioned existence gives us some sense of its actuality as we strive to transcend the limitations of our temporal being. It will be helpful, I believe, to quote at some length Herman Bavinck's discussion of the subject in his *Gereformeerde Dogmatiek*, II (1908), pp. 152–154:

> The essence of time lies in the fact . . . that it contains a succession of moments. There is in time an earlier, a now and a later. From this it follows that time is the existence-form of all that is created, and is an essential part of all that is finite. To say time is to say movement, change, measurability, countability, limitation, finitude, creature. Time is the duration of creaturely being.
>
> For this reason there can be no time in God. He is what he is, from eternity to eternity. . . . He is not a becoming but an eternal being. He has neither beginning nor end, but also no earlier and later. He cannot be measured or counted in duration . . . . The eternity of God is therefore to be thought of as an eternal present, without past or future . . . .
>
> At the same time, God's eternity may not be thought of as an eternal standing still, as an immovable moment of time. It is *one* with God's being and therefore it is a fulness of being . . . . There is an essential distinction between time and eternity, but there is also analogy and relationship, so that eternity can dwell in and be active in time . . . . God, the eternal, is the only absolute cause of time. For that reason time has no existence in itself; it is a continual becoming which rests in unchangeable being. It is God who in his eternai power bears and upholds time in the whole of its existence and in each moment of that existence. God pervades all time and every moment of time with his eternity. He does not himself thereby become temporal, is not subject to time, measure or number. He remains eternal and dwells in eternity. But he uses time to reveal eternal thoughts and virtues in it. He makes time render service to eternity and thus reveals himself to be the king of the ages. (Translation mine)

There is something unquestionably appealing in Bavinck's view, but, in the end, what can one do with it? To ask only one question: How must we understand the conception of an "eternal present"? If there is no past and no future, what is the meaning of "present"? If there is neither beginning nor end, what is the meaning of middle? It is easy on the basis of "some evidence" to draw the "conclusion" that there is no "when" in God's decree, but where does that leave us? This question is all the more pertinent when we consider in which way Dort *did* introduce the "when" question.

Acknowledging that there was no temporal sequence in the decrees, that God's entire decree with all its component parts eternally stood full-blown in the mind of God, the theology regnant at Dort nevertheless dealt fully with the *logical order* of the decrees in the mind of God, and this logical order was definitely of a causal nature. To this emphatic element in the thinking of Dort the committee report makes no reference.

There were two decretal theologies present at the Synod of Dort. Their distinguishing difference related to the logical order of the decrees in God's mind. Specifically, the point of divergence between the two positions was this: Did the decree to elect and reprobate *precede* or *follow upon* the decree to "permit" the fall in point of logical priority? I shall call these positions the pre-fall and the post-fall theologies (and theologians) respectively. The pre-fall theology was first on the scene. It stated that from eternity God decreed to glorify himself by bringing into being an elect humanity to demonstrate his mercy and a reprobate humanity to manifest his justice. To effectuate this end he decreed to create the world and humankind in it; he then decreed to "permit" the fall of man in Adam, and thereupon he decreed to institute the process of salvation whereby the elect would be brought to salvation, and the reprobate by their exclusion from it to their destined end.

The post-fall theology of the decrees of God constituted a reaction to the bald and apparently cold-blooded view of God presented by the pre-fall theology. Did God create humankind to bring elect and reprobate into being? The post-fall theologians sought to protect God against this aspersion and therefore juggled the order of the decrees as follows: God first decreed to create the world and humankind; thereupon he decreed to "permit" the fall (but "efficaciously" so that it would be certain to happen), and then decreed to elect some people to eternal life and leave others to the consequences of the misery into which they had "wilfully cast themselves." Finally, he decreed to initiate the process of redemption of the elect.

The difference between the two views is one of words only. The post-fall *as well as* the pre-fall school of thought sets the history of both salvation and reprobation in what may be called fluid concrete: concrete, because the decreed end is as certain to eventuate in the post-fall as in the pre-fall view; fluid, because the post-fall view involves history with all its changes, convolutions, and uncertainties, as does the pre-fall position.

The elimination of the temporal "When" from the decrees of Dort, therefore, changes nothing. When the reprobate are born they are born into this cycle of eventuation in which the decrees of God are realized in keeping with the "sovereign, most just, irreprehensible, and unchangeable good pleasure" of the divine purpose. Uncreated eternity has priority over and is determinative of created time. This is certainly Bavinck's emphasis. The committee would not deny this with respect to God's sovereign good pleasure of election in eternity. It can therefore not well have a contrary position with respect to reprobation, *especially not* in view of its distinctive and emphatic view that reprobation is no more than an "aspect," a "facet," of election.

The Bible is a religious, not a theological, much less a philosophical book. In it eternity is not set forth as a timeless concept but as part of the *mysterium tremendum* with which God has clothed himself. He condescends to disclose the mystery of his eternity to us in the only terms we can understand, namely our time-conditioned existence. "Before the mountains were brought forth, or ever thou hadst formed the earth and the world, from everlasting to everlasting thou art God" (Ps. 90:2); ". . . before Abraham was, I am" (John 8:58); ". . . Father, glorify thou me in thy own presence with the glory which I had with thee before the world was made" (John 17:5); and many similar passages. The Canons themselves speak of eternity in this way: ". . . as He has chosen His own from eternity in Christ, so He calls them effectually in time" (III-IV/10); ". . . who were from eternity chosen to salvation . . . and having faithfully preserved them even to the end, should at last bring them . . . to . . . His own presence forever" (II/8). Even the committee in less strained argument speaks in this way: "It should not be overlooked that the Canons begin with history—not with the eternal decrees of God, not with the decisions of God from before the foundation of the world, but with our actual, historical, human condition" (pp. 517–518).

4. IS GOD THE DEFICIENT CAUSE OF SIN?

Whatever our understanding of eternity may be, it cannot be doubted that, according to the teaching of Dort, all people who have ever lived, who live now, and who are yet to be born enter life *either* as elect *or* as reprobate. No one ever *becomes* elect in time and no one ever *becomes* reprobate in time.

As we have seen, reprobation is the result of a decree that proceeds from God's sovereign good pleasure and is therefore unconditioned by demerit in any degree. The decree consists of the three inseparable constituent elements of the reprobate being left in the common misery, being denied the gift of faith and the grace of conversion, and being condemned and punished forever for their unbelief and sin. This decree, although absolutely immutable, nevertheless adapts its execution to the realities of history. It is in the course of man's historical existence with all its innumerable cross-currents and events, forces, and circumstances that the elect are irresistibly led to salvation and the reprobate inescapably to condemnation and punishment.

In Reformed theology the fate of the reprobate is made to appear as a wholly just punishment for the sin into which they had wilfully plunged themselves. All have sinned in Adam and therefore all are guilty by virtue of their relationship to Adam. Out of this totally guilty humanity God was pleased to save the elect. The others he was pleased to leave in their sin and suffer the consequences of their disobedience. Was this not just? Was this not fair? Was not Adam free not-to-sin? With what right can we question the justice of God's rejection of them? Do those who sin in life not do so voluntarily? Have they not rejected God in unbelief and disobedience? As the study committee asks, "So can we then say that God rejects those who reject him? Most emphatically we can" (p. 521).

Things are not, however, all that simple. Before people could reject God in history God had determined eternally to "permit" them to fall into sin, and he had subsequent to that rejected a segment of the human race by the decree of reprobation. This rejection was not only unilateral in the most absolute sense of the word; it also took place when humankind did not yet exist, and most importantly of all, it was a rejection that arose solely out of God's "good pleasure." Dort rejects indignantly the idea that "God, by a mere arbitrary act of his will, without the least respect or view to any sin, has predestinated the greatest part of the world to eternal damnation, and has created them for this very purpose" (Conclusion, pp. 521, 522). Remarkably, indignation changes almost to veneration when we make a few substitutions drawn from the Canons themselves in the charge that is here rejected. For "mere arbitrary act of his will" read "His sovereign good pleasure"; for "has predestinated the greatest part of the world to eternal damnation" read "others passed by in the eternal decree . . . whom God has decreed to leave in the common misery"; and for "has created them for this very purpose" read "for the declaration of his justice to condemn and punish them forever." When things are said in this way the calumny of the critics becomes the "unspeakable comfort" of holy and pious souls (I/6).

This reprobation, we must remember, took place when the world was not yet, when no human being existed. Even the committee with its no-when kind of thinking says of the irrevocability of this decree,

> . . . it would seem to be an implication of the teaching of the Canons on reprobation, plus their teaching on the nature of our fallen condition, that for a person who never comes to faith it was in fact always impossible that he would. (p. 533)

We must also take a somewhat closer look at the divine decree to "permit" the fall into sin that preceded the decree of reprobation in the "logical order" of all reprobation theology. It may seem strange to the thoughtful reader that the God who created the heavens and the earth and declared his work to be "very good" (Gen. 1:31) should promulgate a decree that man be permitted to fall. Moreover, this permission was not a neutral factor on which man could act as he pleased. It was, says Professor Louis Berkhof, a decree which in permitting sin rendered it certain. According to Berkhof, Reformed theologians are

> averse to the statement that God *willed* sin, and substitute for it the assertion that he *permitted* it . . . . They speak of the decree respecting sin as a *permissive* decree, but with the distinct understanding that this decree rendered the entrance of sin into the world a certainty. (*Reformed Dogmatics*, I: 108, 109)

The study committee was fully aware of this background in Dort's thinking, as is evident from their historical survey (pp. 504–505), but it plays no role at all in their exposition of Dort's teaching on reprobation.

It is plain to the commonsensical reader, be he believer or unbeliever, that:

> when behind the original sin of Adam stands an immutable decree that he shall fall permissively but inevitably,

when an eternal divine decree declares that the reprobate shall be left in the misery into which they have plunged themselves,

when that same eternal decree declares that the reprobate shall never receive the gift of faith or the grace of conversion,

when the eternal decrees that are effectuated in time have an irrevocable status of unchangeableness,

when their entire life speeds the reprobate on to a condemnation and punishment that they can escape no more than they can escape their own shadow,

when throughout all the states of reprobation there runs the purpose of the glorification of God as willed by God,

and when all this arises out of God's inscrutable "good pleasure" from which any cause of sin, unbelief, or demerit of any kind is totally and completely excluded,

then, according to such teaching, God cannot escape accountability for man's sin and unbelief.

Both Dort and the committee reject this conclusion emphatically and repeatedly. Nevertheless, there is a substantial difference between Dort's denial and the committee's denial. The Dortian denial is *absolute*. It has no qualifications. Article 5 of Chapter I of the Canons puts the matter plainly:

The cause or guilt of this unbelief as well as of all other sins is no wise in God, but in man himself . . . .

And again, in Article 15,

And this is the decree of reprobation, which by no means makes God the Author of sin (the very thought of which is blasphemy) . . . .

The absolute element in Article 5 lies in the expression, "is no wise in God," and in Article 15 in "which by no means makes God . . . ." The denial of God's responsibility for sin is not argued nor commented on; it is simply *stated*.

The study committee's denial is emphatic, but is far from absolute. It writes,

Isn't God, after all, the *cause* of the unbelief of those who in fact have no faith? . . . To this Dort repeatedly says "No"; the cause lies in the sinful condition of man himself, and of his sinful condition God is not the cause. God is the cause of unbelief only in the sense of "deficient causality." (p. 520)

And later

. . . the Canons teach that this passing over is not a *cause* of their unbelief and impiety, except in the sense of "deficient cause." (p. 522)

It should be noted again that here the committee is not in the first place expressing its own views; it is presenting what it conceives *Dort* to teach. The Canons' cause-in-no-wise and cause-by-no-means becomes in the committee's version of their teaching cause-by-deficient-action. Now it would appear that a deficient cause is a cause. In the first quotation the committee actually makes that statement: "God is the cause of unbelief . . . ." followed by a qualification of that statement, "only in the sense of 'deficient causality.' " But the qualification does not deny the fact of cause. The concept of deficient cause in this context means that God could have prevented the fall, but did not. On the contrary, God decreed to "permit" the fall, and that in such a way that it would most certainly happen. When one puts carefree children to play dangerously close to certain destruction and does not seek to prevent them from meeting that fate, and it comes upon them, is he not properly considered guilty of contributing to, if not guilty of, the disaster? Is such a person not certain to be charged with culpable neglect? Must not the same be said of God's role in the origin of sin and unbelief, whether according to Dort or according to the committee?

In examining various theories about God's relationship to sin, Herman Bavinck wrote about deficient cause as a possible answer to the problem. He said:

> The concept of permission is without the slightest force against the accusation that God is the author of sin, for he who permits a person to sin and be lost, while he is in position to prevent it, is as guilty as one who incites him to sin. (Ibid., p. 403)

There is in the committee's presentation of Dort's position a certain theological simplicity that is altogether disturbing. The vast and inescapable involvement of God in the sin of man seems suddenly to cease to exist because Dort denies in words that God is the author of sin. But, one asks: What *about* those decrees? Can man somehow escape their power? Can man frustrate the intent and foreordination of God? Do simple denials in a court of law annul overwhelming evidence in the very writing of the accused? For Dort based its teaching of reprobation on what it considered to be the explicit testimony of Scripture.

It may seem to some to be arrogant and presumptuous to speak of citing God before the bar of humankind. But it is not. We are made in God's image. The conception of right and wrong, however deeply distorted and frequently misapplied, is common to all human beings because we are made in God's image. Again and again the Bible compares God to a human being—a father, a mother, a king, a judge, a teacher, a shepherd—and moves from what such a person would or would not do to what God would or would not do. Indeed, Isaiah presents God as inviting Israel to judge him:

> And now, O inhabitants of Jerusalem and men of Judah,
>   judge, I pray you, between me and my vineyard.
> What more was there for me to do for my vineyard,
>   that I have not done in it?
> When I looked for it to yield grapes, why did it yield
>   wild grapes? (5:3–4)

Were God so to speak in the final judgment of the reprobate, could not some clever theologically versed victim of God's "good pleasure" reply to the intricacies of deficient causality with, "You could have elected me"? Where would that leave the righteous Judge of all the earth? If he replied, "It was my sovereign good plesure not so to do," the clever one could still taunt him with, "Then what's the point of asking what more you could have done?"

Scripture, like Dort, denies God's causing the evil that is in the world, but unlike Dort it does not propose an intricate system of divine self-exoneration. It does not give a rationale for the existence of irrationality. It regards evil as a horrible, incomprehensible reality that is not to be explained but is to be vanquished, undone, and put away forever and ever. This was done by Christ on the cross, and the announcement of this is the gospel.

There is a surprising statement in the study committee report that casts remarkable light on the nature of its thinking in this matter in relation to the message of Scripture. In the course of its exegesis of Romans 9–11 it states:

> These chapters clearly affirm that God has graciously chosen certain people (both Jews and Gentiles) to be recipients of salvation in Jesus Christ . . . . These are referred to as a remnant . . . . But what about those not chosen for salvation? Paul does not say in this discussion that God rejected them. One could say that God's not choosing some is tantamount to his rejection of them. Paul, however, does not specifically draw that implication. Paul continually stresses that, whereas election is by grace . . . , the condition of the nonelect results from their unbelief . . . . On the contrary, God has maintained a gracious attitude even toward the disobedient ones . . . . (p. 538)

Clearly the committee, like Dort, was unwilling to accept the silence of Scripture as an admonition to refrain from making God speak where revelation has not spoken. It reinforced the arrogance of Dort and supported its own religious and theological boldness by refusing to stop where Paul stopped. Even in the day-to-day earthly concerns of life it is extremely hazardous to interpret silence. How much more does reticence become us when we face the silences of Scripture about the ways of God and the eternal destiny of men?

Basically, it is this reticence that the gravamen asked the church to adopt in the matter of reprobation. Without asking this explicitly, it invited the church to return to the simplicity of her chief and weekly-used confession, the Heidelberg Catechism:

> 54. Q. What do you believe concerning the *holy catholic Church*?
>   A. That the Son of God, out of the whole human race, from the beginning to the end of the world, gathers, defends, and preserves for Himself, by His Spirit and Word, in the unity of the true faith, a Church chosen to everlasting life; and that I am, and forever shall remain, a living member thereof.

This is all that the Heidelberg Catechism has to say about election, and there is not a word in it about reprobation. Is this not far healthier than to have an involved confessional statement about reprobation for which it is officially admitted that the historic biblical grounds adduced for it are invalid? Is it not better to be credally silent than to have an imposing confessional declaration that we neither preach nor teach nor openly discuss when we have the very example of Paul in Romans 9–11 to support credal silence? The Heidelberg Catechism takes election out of the individualistic context in which Dort places it and relates it in first order to the community of the church whose members participate in the election of the body, leaving itself unencumbered by a doctrine of reprobation that has no foundation in Scripture, has no hold on the hearts and minds of believers, and can be maintained only by specious theological formulations that cannot bear the light of scriptural analysis.

5. REPROBATION AND SCRIPTURE

According to the now familiar Article 15 of Chapter I of the Canons,

> holy Scripture most especially highlights this eternal and undeserved grace of our election in that it further bears witness that not all men have been chosen, but that some have not been chosen, or have been passed by in God's eternal election . . . .

What is to be noted here is that Scripture "bears witness" to what is theologically and credally called reprobation. *What is this witness?*

In the history of Reformed theology few have questioned the nature of this witness. It consisted of a number of passages that individually and collectively were considered to be infallible witnesses to the truth of the doctrine. Especially appealed to were chapters 9–11 of Paul's letter to the Romans: "As it is written, 'Jacob I loved, but Esau I hated' " (9:13); "So then he has mercy upon whomever he wills, and he hardens the heart of whomever he wills" (9:18); "Has the potter no right over the clay, to make out of the same lump one vessel for beauty and another for menial use?" (9:21); "What if God, desiring to show his wrath and to make known his power, has endured with much patience the vessels of wrath fitted for destruction . . ." (9:22); "Israel failed to obtain what it sought. The elect obtained it, but the rest were hardened . . ." (11:7). Other verses express similar thoughts: ". . . for they stumble because they disobey the word, as they were destined to do" (I Pet. 2:8); ". . . I thank thee, Father, Lord of heaven and earth, that thou has hidden these things from the wise and understanding and revealed them to babes; yea, Father, for such was thy gracious will" (Matt. 11:25–26). These and still other passages formed the specifically biblical basis for the doctrine of reprobation.

True, human reason has played a large role in support of the doctrine; it is reasonable to say that if God did not elect everyone then he must have rejected some. Such reasoning constitutes what has been called "the logic of the situation." It is significant, however, that such support or defense of the doctrine of reprobation has always stood in a context of specifically biblical, that is, textual, witness. The gravamen study committee gives a good idea of how large this textual witness was. It presents a separate section entitled "Scripture Passages Adduced by the Delegates to the Synod of Dort." There are more than a hundred passages that are subsumed under twelve different aspects of the doctrine. These aspects are:

1. That God has determined not to elect some people but to leave some in their sins and not to have mercy on them in Christ.

2. That God does not give faith, repentance, and salvation to some.

3. That some have not been given to Christ.

4. That certain ones were previously consigned to condemnation.

5. That reprobation has been decreed from eternity.

6. That the cause for reprobation (or preterition) lies in the free will or good pleasure of God.

7. That the decree of preterition is unchangeable.

8. That the decree of preterition is not a cause of sin nor of condemnation.

9. That those who are condemned are condemned because of their sins.

10. That God permits the reprobates to walk in their own ways.

11. That the reprobates in various ways and stages reject the gospel which is preached to them.

12. That the end of reprobation is not the perdition of the reprobates but the honor and glory of God. (pp. 534–535)

Here everyone who is at all familiar with the Reformed theology of reprobation feels on familiar ground. When Dort therefore speaks of "express testimony" or of Scripture's "especially highlighting the grace of election in that it further bears witness that not all men have been chosen . . ." we have a very good idea indeed of what the Canons have in mind. The Canons mean, and the delegates meant, a large number of passages that are considered to teach *directly* the decree of reprobation as we have presented it in Chapter 2.

The study committee regards the matter quite differently, however. And of necessity it had to. In its view, reprobation is no more than a "facet" or an "aspect" of election. Indeed, reprobation *is not a decree at all* in the sense in which election is a decree. The committee therefore declares with great emphasis that the passages understood by Dort to teach reprobation *are not*

a group of passages which independently prove the doctrine of reprobation, but rather a group of Scripture passages which affirm that *election is limited*. The fathers of Dort were convinced that this was the way *the Bible taught* the doctrine of election. (p. 527)

All that formerly was regarded as a witness to reprobation in distinction from election has now been absorbed into the *one decree of election*. In this one decree that which Dort called "the decree of reprobation" is now "aspect of," "facet of," "involved in" the doctrine of election. And the committee is "convinced" that this is what the fathers of Dort really meant when they spoke of "reprobation."

On what is this "conviction" based? The committee makes no effort to show *how* the many passages adduced by the delegates as teaching reprobation in fact teach election—that is, "limited election." What the committee does undertake to do is to show how *it* understands the Bible to teach "limited election." To wit:

> How can we show that Scripture teaches that election is limited? . . . The Old Testament describes Yahweh (or Jehovah) as choosing the following: Abraham, Jacob, Moses, Aaron, the Levites, Joshua, Gideon, Samson, Samuel, Saul, David, Solomon, Elisha, Amos, Isaiah, Jeremiah, Ezekiel, Zerubbabel, and others. In each case, the choosing of one person involved the *passing by* of other persons . . . as an inherent aspect of the choosing . . . . In choosing Abraham . . . , God did not choose Nahor . . . . In choosing David, God passed by Eliab . . . and all the other sons of Jesse.
>
> . . . God also chose Abraham's descendants to be his "chosen people." This means that other people were not selected to be God's "chosen people." (p. 548)

It is difficult to surmise how the committee came to compare God's non-choosing of X number of people and nations with the Dortian conception of reprobation. It would seem that pedantic dictionary literalness replaced the Bible as the committee's teacher, as Aristotle's "deficient cause" replaced the silence of Scripture concerning the cause of sin and unbelief. For there are great differences between God's choosing and non-choosing as reported in the Old Testament and God's electing and reprobating as reported in Dort. God's choosing of the individuals mentioned, each for his particular task, eliminated no one from the human race, destined no one to eternal perdition, cut off no one from his people or nation, denied to no one the blessings of God's covenant. As for Israel, her task was to prepare the coming of the Messiah that through him salvation might be open to the whole world. God's promise to Abraham was, "In you all the families of the earth will be blessed." The committee fully recognizes these things (noted in the gravamen) but nevertheless stands unbendingly on its dictionary definition:

> All this is true. But the fact still remains that God has one chosen people, and that chosen nation was Israel, not the Philistines, or the Edomites, or the Egyptians. In choosing the descendants of Abraham

as the chosen people, God passed by the other nations . . . . This remains true even though it be granted that Abraham's descendants were chosen in order to be a blessing to all the nations of the world. (p. 549)

If this indeed be true, how is it to be understood that Abraham's descendants were also chosen to be a curse for all the nations? How can election as the highest expression of grace and blessing be at the same time a manifestation of reprobation through an essential "aspect" or "facet" of God's electing love? What madness drives theologians to propose and synods to adopt such absurdity?

The report cites some New Testament passages to illustrate that God's "electing to eternal life is done in such a way that some are elected while others are passed by" (p. 549):

"All that the Father gives me will come to me; and him who comes to me I will in no wise cast out . . . ." (John 6:37)

"I do not pray for these only, but also for those who believe in me through their word . . . ." (John 17:20)

"And when the Gentiles heard this, they were glad . . . and as many as were ordained to eternal life believed." (Acts 13:48)

"We know that in everything God works for good with those who love him . . . . For those whom he foreknew he also predestined . . . . [and] called . . . [and] justified . . . [and] glorified." (Rom. 8:28-30) (pp. 549-550)

There is not even a whisper in these passages about those who are "passed by." Here again the ingrained rationalism of the committee is unable to accept the silence of Scripture concerning the cause of unbelief. The mystery of unbelief that Scripture nowhere resolves must be penetrated by its book-learning logic.

Such, then, is the evidence for Dort's doctrine of reprobation, according to the committee. This "evidence" is not presented as the *committee's* evidence of *its* version of reprobation; rather, this is the kind of scriptural evidence Dort is alleged to have had in mind. Both the committee and the synods of 1980 and 1981 strenuously resist the charge that the Canons have in any manner been revised. The passages quoted above can of course be almost indefinitely extended. What the committee means to say is that the biblical evidence for reprobation *is* election. To say election is to say that "aspect," that "facet" which is "involved" in all election, namely "passing over." That and only that is what Dort is alleged to have meant by reprobation.

I shall not ask whether this is a fair presentation of Dort or of the historic Reformed understanding of reprobation. I shall rather ask: What theologian in the Christian Reformed Church will undertake to defend the committee report and its synodical endorsement against the charge of unqualified distortion of the teaching of the Canons of Dort?

We have seen the character of the biblical evidence for the Christian Reformed synodical "new look" in Dort's reprobation theology. I shall close this chapter by citing the evidence for the doctrine of reprobation, as Dort understood it, from the writings of one with whose competence and authority to speak for Dort no one in the Christian Reformed Church will argue, namely the late Professor Louis Berkhof. In his *Reformed Dogmatics* (I:100), he cites the following Scripture references as teaching the doctrine of reprobation as understood in the Reformed tradition:

> *Rom. 9:13* As it is written, "Jacob I loved, but Esau I hated."
>
> *9:17* For the Scripture says to Pharaoh, "I have raised you up for the very purpose of showing my power in you, so that my name may be proclaimed in all the earth."
>
> *9:18* So then he has mercy on whom he wills, and he hardens the heart of whomever he wills.
>
> *9:21* Has the potter no right over the clay, to make out of the same lump one vessel for beauty and another for menial use?
>
> *9:22* What if God, desiring to show his wrath and to make known his power, has endured with much patience the vessels of wrath made for destruction . . . .
>
> *11:7* What then? Israel failed to obtain what it sought. The elect obtained it, but the rest were hardened . . . .
>
> *Jude 4* For admission has been secretly gained by some who long ago were designated for this condemnation, ungodly persons who pervert the grace of our God into licentiousness and deny our only Master and Lord, Jesus Christ.
>
> *I Pet. 2:8* . . . "A stone that will make men stumble, a rock that will make them fall"; for they stumble because they disobey the word, as they were destined to do.

It is precisely this kind of evidence that the gravamen showed as *not* teaching reprobation when analyzed in its several contexts. The committee has judged that my exegesis is correct. But it has also said that my exegesis is "irrelevant." Why? Because Dort does not teach what I allege it to teach. Perhaps I cannot read Calvin and the Canons and Bavinck and Kuyper and Berkouwer and Berkhof. I am not, however, persuaded of this, for my reading is wholly at one with the Reformed consensus. The more likely situation is that there is something seriously awry in the gravamen study committee's reporting of Dort and the Reformed consensus.

CHAPTER 4

THEOLOGY BY PARLIAMENTARY PROCEDURE

In receiving my gravamen for adjudication in 1977 the synod of the Christian Reformed Church committed itself to *examine* and *judge* its merits as required by the Form of Subscription. In order to do this effectively, it appointed a nine-man, three-year study committee with the following mandate:

> . . . to receive the reactions of individuals, consistories, and classes, to study the gravamen . . . in the light of Scripture, and to advise the Synod of 1980 as to the cogency of the gravamen and how it should further be dealt with by synod. (p. 486)

The committee consisted of three professors of theology, three ministers, and three laymen. One of the laymen was a professor of philosophy and the other two were educators. Its appointment was received very favorably in the church, and not least by myself.

To this must be added a further weighty consideration. The Synod of 1976 had by its revision of the Form of Subscription opened the way for the entire church to discuss publicly the pro's and con's of any gravamen. She would therefore presumably avail herself of this freedom to discuss a particularly sensitive area in the credal witness of the church.

My expectation that the church would come to grips with the issues posed by the gravamen in a significant and helpful way soon dissipated. Public concern could hardly have been expressed more minimally than was the case between June 1977 and June 1980. A few articles appeared in church papers; I was invited to do some speaking here and there; I took part in a substantial debate, and there may well have been discussions of which I am not aware. But the whole, such as it was, can hardly be said to have made an impact on the church. The faculties of Calvin College and Seminary were silent. The ministry, with a few exceptions, showed no interest whatever.

The study committee soon became an anonymous body working behind closed doors that gave no indication in which direction it was moving. It invited me to meet with it in September

1978. As the committee report states, "At one session the committee had an extensive discussion with Dr. Boer about the meaning and purpose of his gravamen." At the time, the committee had not crystallized any of its far-reaching positions. The meeting was a pleasant one. Each member asked me a question to which I responded. I recall only one question that significantly bore on the issue before the committee, and that was not pursued after my response to it. After that I was never again approached by the committee with respect to any questions it might have relative to the gravamen.

As the months went by I could not but wonder why I had been invited to meet with the committee in the first place. Why did it not call me in when the problems that attended their understanding of the gravamen arose and required clear answers? That these apprehensions were justified becomes clear on reading the report. In a crucial section the committee's wonderings about an important point in the gravamen are expressed thus:

> When we first read these words of Boer, it may indeed seem that . . . . Yet, on closer reading, it looks as if . . . . Thus it seems that, according to his position . . . . So far as we can tell, this, on Boer's view, is part of . . . . Could it possibly be Boer's view, however, that . . . ? Dr. Boer, so far as we can tell, does believe that . . . ? Could it be that Boer thinks . . . ? Could it be that in his protest . . . ?
>
> We say that this is *possibly* how Dr. Boer is thinking. If so, our reply is . . . . (pp. 531, 532)

The committee's "reply" finally cut the Gordian knot of my allegedly obscure thought by making me say what the whole gravamen was written to deny. Meanwhile, I was at all times resident in Grand Rapids where the committee met and as close as the nearest telephone or a ten-minute drive in my car. Such a call never came, and that is regrettable. After all, the committee and I were not standing in an adversary relationship to each other. Presumably we were both interested in the truth of things. In no area of the church's life is it more necessary to live out our confession of the communion of saints than in the resolution of credal and theological problems.

Toward the end of 1979 another concern of even larger dimension was beginning to disturb me. Until then, there had been no doubt in my mind that the study committee's report would be referred to the churches for study before its adjudication by the synod. But was this supposition warranted? The more I reflected on the indifferent attitude to the gravamen in the church and on the committee's perfunctory meeting with me, the more I wondered whether the committee would seek adjudication by the Synod of 1980. On January 16, 1980, I therefore addressed a communication to the study committee, the burden of which was:

> It is my very sincere hope that the Synod of 1980 will take no action on your report . . . . There should be fully adequate time for the denomination as a whole to evaluate the fruit of your work. The Synod of 1976 . . . stipulated that
>> A revision of the confessions shall not be adopted by synod until the whole church membership has had adequate opportunity to consider it. *Acts*, 1976, p. 70
> Public reflection on the gravamen has been disappointingly limited. The CRC theological community has virtually ignored it. It is my hope that your report will stimulate such reflection between April 1980 and June 1981. There can be no doubt that the . . . report should now form the central focus of consideration.

In his response the secretary did not openly deny the request, but its impact was negative. This led me to address a second communication to the committee on February 6 in which I reinforced the first letter by quoting further from the Church Order decision of the Synod of 1976:

> . . . when the constituted synod declares the matter to be legally before it for action, all signers of the Form of Subscription shall be free to discuss it with the whole church until adjudicated by synod. *Acts*, p. 69

Here the matter rested until the Agenda for the Synod of 1980 was distributed. The final line of the last page of the report, under *Recommendations* shocked me thoroughly. It read:

> 5. That synod discharge the committee.

In parliamentary language this meant only one thing—that the committee expected (in effect, requested) the synod, only seven weeks away, to adjudicate the gravamen. Were the synod to postpone adjudication to a later year the committee would have to stay in existence to collate church responses and to present these and defend its report before the adjudicating synod. It judged, therefore, that the Synod of 1980 would be competent (in the juridical sense of that word) to *examine* and *judge* the gravamen in the light of its report. I cannot accept that the committee genuinely believed that the Synod of 1980 would have that competence. Admittedly, in any doctrinal adjudication a synod is heavily dependent on the work of its study committee. This dependence, however, may never assume the form of rubber-stamping a committee's advice. But how could the Synod of 1980 conceivably adjudicate the gravamen without abdicating both its responsibility and its self-respect?

The Synod of 1980 faced a printed Agenda of 435 pages, not just one big issue on the doctrine of reprobation. All of synod's members had special committee work for which to prepare, and all of them had their several responsibilities in office, school, factory, church, on the farm, and at home. It is my very considered judgment that not even the synodical advisory committee was in this short time able to get its mind around this exceedingly complex report.

When I expressed my disappointment to members of the committee and to others, a common reply was, "But didn't the church have three years to study the gravamen?" This quite ignores the fact that there had been nothing in the gravamen that prepared the reader for entertaining such new ideas of the study committee report as reprobation being an "aspect" or "facet" of election; the downgrading of the specifically decretal element in the decree of reprobation; God's being the "deficient cause" of sin and unbelief; the alleged "irrelevance" of the historic scriptural basis for the doctrine of reprobation to Dort's understanding of it; and the committee's elimination of the "when" element in God's decrees.

After the publication of the synodical Agenda, therefore, I again, in a letter dated April 24, called the attention of the committee to the provisions of the Church Order governing the adjudication of a gravamen and asked them as yet to cancel the recommendation that it be discharged. I further wrote:

> With what right can the committee, in the light of these clear provisions, recommend in this indirect but undeniable way that its report is none of the church's concern? . . .
>
> The entire purpose of the rules of 1976 ws to eliminate hierarchicalism from the ecclesiastical adjudication of confessional-revision

gravamina. Your recommendation that synod discharge your committee proposes in effect that the hierarchicalism that was eliminated in 1976 be introduced again through the back door in 1980 . . . .

For these reasons, and in the interest of unabridged implementation of Church Order procedures with respect to the present gravamen, I request the committee to withdraw this recommendation from its report.

In a telephone response to this letter the secretary of the committee informed me that no revisions were being proposed. It is technically true that the committee made no explicit proposals for revision. It held its report to be a faithful exposition of what Dort said and meant. But does this ring true? Was the committee not factually proposing a wholly new version of Dort's teaching on reprobation for acceptance by synod?

There was one member of the committee—regrettably, only one—who had a conscience in the matter. On April 28 he wrote a letter to the forthcoming synod which spoke a message that was loud and clear. From it I excerpt the following:

The time between the publication of the Agenda and the meeting of Synod is only some two months—a very short time indeed. Furthermore, only a very tiny proportion of the members of the denomination will have an opportunity to see the Agenda during that time; and the delegates to Synod can by no means concentrate all their attention on this one report. In short, only a very few members of the CRC will have a chance to read the report before Synod, and most of them who do will not be able to give it more than a cursory reading. Though the committee argues that sufficient case has not been presented in the gravamen for altering the Canons, its argument for that conclusion involves the repudiation of many common misreadings of the Canons and the endorsement of fresh lines of exegesis. Accordingly, the argumentation of the report as a whole will take some time for the church to digest.

For these reasons I think it is a *profound mistake* to determine the issue at this Synod. A momentous topic involving controversial issues and fresh interpretations must not be decided on basis of brief and cursory reflection by a few men. That would be the worst kind of hierarchicalism. It would be a disservice to the committee, which after all was given a three year rather than the customary two year mandate, to Dr. Boer, and to the church as a whole.

Meanwhile, Classis Grand Rapids East endorsed an overture from the First Christian Reformed Church of Grand Rapids requesting the deferring of a decision on the gravamen. It stated:

For purposes of adjudication the study committee report is as important as the gravamen. The study of the church as a whole climaxes in the study committee's work. The time elapsing between the appearance of the Agenda for synod and the convening of synod hardly provides opportunity for the forming of an adequate judgment on the part of the delegates. The church membership as a whole will not have had an opportunity at all to do justice to the study of it.

When the synod convened I was given opportunity to meet with the gravamen advisory committee. I requested it to recommend that the report of the study committee be referred to the churches for study with a view to adjudication by a later synod and gave reasons for this. My plea to this committee was no more effective than my communications to the gravamen study committee had been. In its advice to synod it endorsed the argument of the study committee report without a whisper of criticism and advised the synod to adopt its recommendations verbatim.

The synodical assembly took up the gravamen question as first order of business on the morning of Tuesday, June 17. At that time of the synodical day public attendance is at its very lowest and the merest scattering of visitors was present in the galleries. The study committee, the synodical advisory committtee, and the synod-in-session, it seemed, were completely of one mind in the resolve to minimize public awareness of the impending adjudication as well as public knowledge and discussion of the study committee report.

The synod, too, was "willing" to hear me. It gave me ten minutes to say what I had to say, at the very beginning of the discussion and without further opportunity to participate in the deliberation that followed. I pointed out the radical changes effected in the teaching of Dort by (1) the removal of the historic biblical basis of reprobation, (2) the downgrading of the decree of reprobation to being an aspect of election, and (3) attribution to Dort of the teaching that God is the "deficient cause" of unbelief. In concluding my remarks to the synod I said:

> I beg the synod not to fall into the hierarchical fallacy of judging that because you have the authority to adjudicate at this time, you also have the right, in the concrete situation, to so do. You are stewards of the integrity of the creeds, you are not owners of their content. I feel that on this specific point both the study committee and the advisory committee have shown a certain pastoral insensitivity which I trust the synod will not endorse.

But adjudicate it did. The synod was not in a mood to listen to the disturbing distinction between having authority and having the right, in a concrete situation, to exercise it. The following two hours were spent on a rambling unfocused discussion in which the synod manifested no noticeable concern to come to grips with the central issues.

The reasons for this lack of concern, I am persuaded, were two. The first is that there was sheer inability on the part of all involved, without exception, to discuss the basic issues *knowledgeably*. It was *impossible* for the members of the synod to master in the short space of seven weeks the true meaning of the study committee report in its relationship to the gravamen.

Second, there was a general desire to get rid of the issue. This was done as decently as the realities of the situation permitted, but it was done. The absence of discussion in the church does not mean that there was an absence of opinion in the church. The art of Christian Reformed churchmanship is to prevent conflicting opinions on sensitive subjects from meeting in open confrontation. The silence in the church on the issue of reprobation arose neither out of indifference to it nor out of lack of knowledge about its character. It arose out of fear to express in public writing what constantly disturbs the conscience and the minds of the informed.

This evasiveness in dealing with issues of moment comes to expression again and again in Christian Reformed history. Consider what has happened in this dimension during the past thirty-five years in synodical handling of theological issues of moment:

1. The complete discontinuance of synodical concern with Professor D. H. Kromminga's gravamen-type (so judged by the Synod of 1945) communication relative to the compatibility of premillennialism with the Reformed Faith, after his decease in April 1947 (lamentable in view of the well-nigh complete indifference in the Christian Reformed Church to the teaching of Scripture on the doctrine of the last things).

2. The curt dismissal of Professor Clarence Boersma's questions about the Belgic Confession, submitted in 1952 and shunted from committee number 1 to committee number 2 to committee number 3 in a nine-word, non-answer in 1961.

3. The failure to take note of the doctrine of reprobation in adjudicating charges against Professor Harold Dekker arising out of his writings in 1963 and 1964 concerning God's redemptive love for all people, on the part of a two-year study committee and the Synod of 1967, when the study committee *mandate* was to consider his views in the light of Scripture *and the creeds*.

4. The synodical acceptance of Report 44 in 1972 on the Nature and Extent of Scriptural Authority in the light of synod's apparent dissatisfaction with Report 36 submitted in 1971, the fundamental principles of which Report 44 openly claimed to maintain.

5. The ambiguous synodical acquiescence in NAPARC's request for CRC commitment to the inerrancy of Scripture, involving a clear Yes and a clear No on one and the same matter.

6. The concluding of synod's concern with the view of Scripture entertained by Dr. A. Verhey, in 1979, in which at 11:45 in the morning of June 20 (after three hours of debate) it voted 78 to 74 *against* a motion to clear him, and at 2 PM of the same day on substantively the same motion (forbidden by the *Rules of Synod*), with words juggled and the addition of a gratuitous "with thanks to God," voted 119 to 33 to clear him.

The action on the reprobation gravamen stands, therefore, in an established pattern of equivocation by synods confronted with controversial theological matters.

On other issues, however, the highest assembly of the Christian Reformed Church is quite capable of responsible action. This it demonstrated on the very day in which it discharged its stewardship of the gospel in the manner described above. Before the synod was a report on dancing that had been occasioned by the covert practice of that amusement in Calvin College residence halls, in what were known as "parties with music." With a solicitude conspicuously absent in its disposition of the gravamen, the synod decided that

> . . . Report 28, "Dance and the Christian Life," [be referred] to the churches for study and evaluation for a period of two years . . . .
> *Grounds*:
> **a.** The study committee requests this study and evaluation.
> **b.** The content and scope of this report warrants serious study, evaluation, and response by the churches.
> **c.** The report addresses an area of life that urgently needs this guidance. (*Acts*, 1980, p. 80.)

It would seem that the "area of life" in the Christian Reformed Church that requires all deacons, elders, ministers, and professors at Calvin College and Seminary to declare in their signing of the Form of Subscription that God by an eternal decree withholds "the gift of faith and the grace of conversion" from a segment of humankind would merit similar concern. Especially would one expect this when it is considered that few if any of the signers give reason to believe that in their hearts they take for truth this gospel-denying declaration. Neither the study committee, nor the advisory committee of synod, nor the synod itself judged it desirable that the defense of this controverted teaching should be laid before the church.

*   *   *

Supported by the council of the First Christian Reformed Church of Grand Rapids but declined by Classis Grand Rapids East, I appealed to the Synod of 1981 the decision of the Synod of 1980 to adjudicate the gravamen before making the report of the study committee known to the church. The ground adduced was that the Synod of 1980 had in substance revised the Canons of Dort by endorsing the report of the study committee and by recommending it to the church as an elucidation of the Canons of Dort. This was in violation of the Church Order as amended by the Synod of 1976: "A revision of the confessions shall not be adopted by synod until the whole church membership has had adequate opportunity to consider it."

The appeal rested on three major considerations:

1. Removal by the Synod of 1980 of the scriptural basis on which Dort rested its doctrine of reprobation and substituting in its place a wholly new scriptural basis in support of the teaching of "limited election";

2. The impermissible reduction of the explicit decretal character of the doctrine of reprobation in the Canons;

3. The attribution to God of being the "deficient cause" of sin and unbelief.

The report of the advisory committee, on basis of which the Synod of 1981 adjudicated the appeal, evinced no theological seriousness, no concern to render a judgment that would stand up in a genuine adjudication. It judged that the Synod of 1980 was "very conscious of the fact that what was recommended and decided was not a revision of the confession." It based its recommendation to reject the appeal on quotations from the incriminated portions of the study committee report. The following, its response to the "deficient cause" thesis, is representative of the treatment:

> However one construes what Report 30 says about deficient cause, it is introduced by this statement about the cause of unbelief: "the cause lies in the sinful condition of man himself, and of this sinful condition God is not the cause." (*Acts*, 1981, p. 104.)

Which simply means that the accused denies the charge that is brought against him, a not uncommon defense of very guilty people in courts of law. The advice completely ignored that a deficient cause *is a cause*.

In any event, it made little difference what the advisory committee said. The synod took up its report at nine o'clock in the evening of its final session. It is common knowledge that at that point in the life of any synod serious deliberation is least likely to occur. I personally witnessed the treatment of the appeal on the floor of synod.

The report of the advisory committee having been previously distributed and read to the synod was thereby before the assembly for debate. At 9:10 a delegate requested serious consideration of the matter on the ground that the action of the Synod of 1980 implied universal infant salvation, a position that had never been taken by the Christian Reformed Church. While this was a theologically valid observation, it did not bear on the matter before the house. Nevertheless, the point was debated until at 9:30 the chairman announced, "break for coffee." At 9:45 an attempt was made to raise the matter again, but this was stopped in its tracks by a delegate's sneeze of such stentorian proportions that for a moment the entire assembly was cast into stunned silence, and then burst out into boisterous laughter which, after abating, started up again to ripple off at last into amused quiescence. The chairman asked if there were further remarks on the motion to adopt the committee's recommendations. There were none. A member called for the question. The vote was taken. It unanimously approved the motion to accept the committee's recommendations, *which had not received the slightest consideration* and which, it is to be feared, few had even read.

Thus came to an end the concern of the synod of the Christian Reformed Church with my gravamen against the doctrine of reprobation as expressed in the Canons of Dort. More specifically, thus came to an end synod's fulfillment of the solemn obligation to *examine* and *judge* my gravamen, which obligation it took upon itself according to the Form of Subscription when, in 1977, it accepted said gravamen for action. In 1980 the synod acted upon the indictment of the gravamen in a context of dark ignorance and parliamentary maneuver; in 1981 it acted on my appeal in a context of complete disregard of my complaint.

What is striking in this demonstration of ecclesiastical bad faith is the unqualified faithfulness to the righteousness of the law in which it was effected. The synod had officially accepted as valid the submission of the gravamen. It had appointed a blue-ribbon study committee to evaluate it. The gravamen was printed in the *Acts of Synod* of 1977. The committee met ten times and its members performed various assignments of homework. The Synod of 1980 had received its report and had committed it for analysis to an advisory committee that had no other assignment than to study it and make recommendations with respect to it. Nearly an entire morning of synod's time was given to a discussion of it. The same correctness was shown in the disposition of my appeal in 1981. Not a single procedural step was omitted. No New Testament pharisee ever fulfilled the law more punctiliously than the synods of 1980 and 1981 observed the law governing the adjudication of a gravamen. Even the Church Order provisions of 1976 had been "observed," for the report of the study committee, far from being viewed as a revision, was declared in 1980 to be an "elucidation of the teaching of the Canons on election and reprobation"; and in 1981 collective unconcern declared that the Synod of 1980 had made clear that its decision "was not a revision of the confession."

What more could I have wished, therefore, that was not given? One thing, and one thing only, without which the entire procedure became a mockery: the life-breath of integrity, the honesty of genuine effort to consider and weigh the complaint of the aggrieved party. The concern of the synods of 1973, 1974, and 1976 genuinely to involve the church in the gravamen process, and the promise of the Synod of 1977 to *examine* and *judge* the gravamen when it received it for action, were callously betrayed by the synods of 1980 and 1981. Not only was the church effectively excluded from knowledge of the study committee's response to the gravamen, but it was adjudicated by a synod that had neither the knowledge nor the understanding requisite for a serious verdict. It endorsed the irresponsibility of the study committee's request for immediate action on its report, and then compounded that disregard for right and law by endorsing the report and recommending it to the church as an "elucidation" of Dort without knowing what it was doing. The Synod of 1981, in the context of appeal, repeated the process utterly.

The Christian Reformed Church holds all her office-bearers strictly accountable for obedience to the Form of Subscription. But when my gravamen was to be adjudicated it was given a polite brush-off by the very synodical authority that had in the act of accepting it in 1977 pledged its word to *examine* and *judge* it according to the very Form of Subscription that it enforces so rigorously upon office-bearers.

If the law of the land were treated with such disdain in a civil court, what anger, what sorrow, what indignation there would be in the community. But where is the shame, where is the indignation in the Christian Reformed Church for the synodical perpetration of a greater wrong—the miscarriage of justice *in the church*, the pillar and ground of the truth, and that in the name of the Lord of the church.

Thus did two Christian Reformed synods discharge their stewardship of the Word of God when they were called upon to weigh evidence against a Reformed credal tradition. Thus did they by means honored neither in heaven nor among people of honorable spirit maintain an orthodoxy that they dare not test. Thus did they apply in the life of the church the once living, now petrified, slogan of the Reformation: *Ecclesia Reformata Semper Reformanda Est.*[1]

---

1. A Reformed church has the duty of always reforming herself.

CHAPTER 5

ELECTION

The cornerstone of the study committee report is the Dortian doctrine of election. From that doctrine are derived the characteristic positions of limited election, God as deficient cause of unbelief, reprobation as a "facet" or "aspect" of and "involved" in election, and the new scriptural basis for what is left of Dort's doctrine of election. In working out its positions the committee never indicated any reservations with respect to the doctrine. Election was the committee's point of departure, its principle for understanding reprobation, the unquestioned teaching from which flowed all its deductions about reprobation.

It is therefore with not a little surprise that we read the far-reaching qualifications which the committee in fact held about the doctrine of election. Having come to the end of its doctrinal argument on basis of which it rejected the gravamen, the committee expressed the following incisive criticism of Dort's central teaching:

> In recommending this disposition of the gravamen we do not wish to be taken as suggesting that the Canons are in every way satisfactory. On the contrary, the Canons confront us not only with inadequacies but with unresolved questions, problems, and tensions. There is, for example, no discussion of the election of Israel and of the church, whereas a balanced treatment of election would surely require attention to that. Likewise, the fact that our election is election *in Christ* does not receive very adequate treatment in the Canons. Again, it has often been suggested in recent years that the Canons think too deterministically about the way in which God grants us his gift of faith. And the Canons apparently see no problem whatsoever in construing the biblical language of "before the foundation of the world" as meaning *from eternity*—that is, from timelessness. Furthermore, it would seem to be an implication of the teaching of the Canons on reprobation, plus their teaching on the nature of our fallen condition, that for a person who never comes to faith, it was in fact always impossible that he would. Yet that seems to be in tension with the genuinely biblical note sounded in III-IV, 8-9, where Dort speaks of the well-meant gospel offer, and of God's desire that those who are called should come to him. Perhaps this is a tension that we must live with if we would adequately reflect the biblical witness. At other points, however, some of which we have mentioned, Dort appears to us to be definitely

> inadequate. Accordingly, in defending the Canons against the Boer gravamen, we are not suggesting that Dort provides an unimprovable theological structure. We are only saying that Boer, on the points at issue, has misinterpreted the Canons. (p. 533)

The statement is carefully hedged. The committee does not want to suggest that the Canons are "in every way satisfactory"; our election in Christ does not receive "adequate treatment"; it "has often been suggested in recent years" that according to the Canons believers receive their faith from God too deterministically. Also, and not least, "it would seem" to be "an implication" of the Canons that for a person who never comes to faith it was in fact always impossible that he would. This "seems to be" in tension with what Dort says elsewhere, and this is a tension that we "perhaps" must live with.

In spite of all seeming, suggestion, implication, and perhaps, it is clear that in the mind of the committee Dort, in respect of the reservations made, is "definitely inadequate." This definite inadequacy focuses especially on election. But election, as Dort viewed it, is the foundation of the whole report and it is the rock from which the doctrine of reprobation is said to be hewn. So if we have a definite inadequacy facing us in the doctrine of election, what must we think of the *derived* view of reprobation that the committee, moreover, has liberally embellished with its own conceptions of what Dort "may well" have meant?

Before considering these matters further, it is appropriate at this point to refer to my position on election insofar as it bears on the gravamen. The study committee has this to say about it:

> Dr. Boer by his own testimony purposely formulated the gravamen with little or no attention given to the doctrine of election. He explicitly states that the gravamen does not call into question the doctrine of election as confessed in the Reformed churches. Yet Dr. Boer asserts that historically election and reprobation have been intimately connected and bound together as correlates and contrasts. If this is indeed true, it would seem that to eliminate the doctrine of reprobation from the church's confession or to declare that doctrine confessionally nonbinding would have some implications for the church's understanding and confession of the doctrine of election. Dr. Boer would have aided the church in its appraisal of his gravamen if he had commented more extensively on the traditional doctrine of election and on his present views regarding that doctrine. (p. 522)

In the gravamen I had written as follows:

> Excluded from the gravamen are any objections to the doctrine of election. I stand wholly committed to the scriptural teaching concerning the sovereignty of God in the salvation of men. (p. 487)

Obviously, my unqualified rejection of the doctrine of reprobation is bound to affect my view of election if only because for me the electing God is seen *not* to be a reprobating God. I therefore did not say that I had no reservations on the Dortian doctrine of election, but that I stand wholly committed to the sovereignty of God in the salvation of men—which I understand to be the basis of election. On this, however, the gravamen does not elaborate. In my judgment the doctrine of reprobation is so patently wrong, so subversive of the gospel of grace, that rejection of it ought not to be conditioned or influenced by any view of election that seeks to be true to Scripture.

What bearing such rejection might have had on the Reformed doctrine of election could have been taken up as the need for this might press itself upon the church once the rejection had taken place. The elimination of the doctrine of reprobation from the body of confessional doctrine would in unpredictable ways have raised religious and theological questions in the life and fellowship of the church. All that the gravamen sought to achieve was the elimination of reprobation as a confessionally binding doctrine, with a view to freeing our reading of the Scriptures, doing our evangelism, pastoring the congregation, and thinking about the saving work of Christ without being burdened by the oppressive encumbrance of reprobation's monstrous distortion of the gospel.

However that may be, the question of the nature of election now stands fully before the church, *and the gravamen did not put it there*. It was put there in first order by the report of the gravamen study committee and, more importantly, officially by the action of the Synod of 1980 when it referred Report 30 to the churches "for elucidation of the teaching of the Canons on election and reprobation" (p. 76).

The report has little to say about election in a direct way. Rather, it seems to assume throughout an understanding of the traditionally held view of election, notably as articulated in the Canons of Dort. If anything, it may be said that the emphasis on reprobation as being implicit in "limited election," on reprobation as a "facet" or "aspect" of election, on God as the "deficient cause" of unbelief sought—in a wholly impermissible

manner—to enlarge the traditional understanding. The whole
effort emphasizes, as hardly anything could, the temptation to
theologize about election by way of logical deduction rather than
by careful study of Dort and exegesis of Scripture. It shows, too,
what happens to theology in the ecclesiastical community when
the theologically trained who are called to that task in the ministry
and in the professorship abdicate that responsibility and leave it
to a panel of presumed "experts" who want their insights to be
acted upon with complete exclusion of the church and with
ignorance enthroned in the adjudicating assembly.

If these things register in the ecclesiastical and theological Christian Reformed mind, the aberration through which we are passing may yet prove to be a cloud with a silver lining.

The long quotation from the study committee report with which
this chapter began is a tribute to the basically religious sensitivity
of the committee as it worked its way through its mandate.
Theology-as-academic-discipline is related to religion-as-human-
experience in the same way in which agriculture is related to
farming. The science of agriculture seeks by means of analysis,
observation, and experiment to lift the elementary activity of
raising crops and livestock to higher levels of productivity.
Similarly, theology endeavors to illuminate and enrich the simple religious understanding of the gospel by systematic reflection
on the content of Scripture, on Christian experience, and on the
history of these in the life of God's people. Every theologian truly
so called is first and foremost a religious being. Theological
interest is acquired; religious concern is native to humans. The
work of the Holy Spirit in the heart of humans is organic in the
sense that it operates in terms of illumining, persuasive, moral,
renewing activity. These modes of operation welcome and benefit
by theological reflection, but they resist a method of theologizing
that violates them. Through his basically religious being the
theologian becomes aware of having overreached himself when
he ventures beyond the bounds set by the Spirit for the exercise
of his theological faculty.

What page 533 of the committee report does is to sound the
alarm, whether instinctively or deliberately, against the encroach-
ment of theology on religion. Our basic religious awareness as
shaped by the gospel cannot permit an intellectual theological
exercise to neutralize the God-given apprehension of truth as it
is mediated to the heart by faith in Christ. The Bible is a religious,

not a theological book. It welcomes theological reflection as a servant of religion; it resists to the death being encased in logical or philosophical straight-jackets.

This is what finally surfaced in the report of the committee. As religious men, molded and formed by God's disclosure of his provision for the redemption of humankind, they sensed that an election that is deterministic in character, that has damnation inherent in God's elective act of grace as a facet or aspect, is not an acceptable way of relating God's salvation to faith and religious experience. They sensed that somehow election is a wholeness that cannot be correctly apprehended by isolating the election of individuals from the election of Israel, of Christ, and of the church. They sensed that there is something that is terribly wrong with a divine predestination that turns the unfeigned invitation to faith and obedience into a formality that can never take hold of one whom God in his eternal decree has designated as reprobate. As men religiously formed by the message of redemptive good news for all people, they rebelled against reprobation's teaching that the call to believe and the duty to believe are not actionable by many to whom the call to faith comes.

The committee did not, however, accept the necessary consequences of this belated insight. It did not occasion a return to theological wholeness and responsibility. Instead of questioning the validity of its use of the election that it now so severely criticizes, the committee endeavored to effect some sort of union between its intellectualistic limited election–reprobation conception and its existential religious revulsion against it. It discerns a "tension" between the inability of the reprobate ever to believe (". . . for a person who never comes to faith, it was in fact always impossible that he would") and the "genuinely biblical note" sounded in Canons III-IV, Articles 8 and 9. These articles read, respectively:

> As many as are called by the gospel are unfeignedly called. For God has most earnestly and truly declared in His Word what is acceptable to Him, namely, that those who are called should come unto Him. He also seriously promises rest of soul and eternal life to all who come to Him and believe.
>
> It is not the fault of the gospel, nor of Christ offered therein, nor of God, who calls men by the gospel and confers upon them various gifts, that those who are called by the ministry of the Word refuse to come and be converted. The fault lies in themselves . . . .

The committee writes:

> Perhaps this is a tension that we must live with if we would adequately
> reflect the biblical witness. (p. 533)

Observe what is happening here: the doctrine of reprobation for
which, by the committee's own admission, there is not a shred
of biblical evidence, is given the same status in biblical authority
as the "genuinely biblical note" sounded in III-IV/8, 9. Each is
to be given equal weight, and when we hold them in the balance
envisioned by the committee we shall "adequately reflect the
biblical witness." But this is theological nonsense. A tension in
the sense in which the committee apparently intends it to be
understood is a relationship between two entities whereby each
both limits and complements the other, as in the relationship
between states' rights and federal authority in the structure of
American government. Obviously, the decree of reprobation and
the unfeigned call of the gospel do not so relate to each other at
all. The true relationship between them can only be described as
one of flat contradiction. There is much in the ways of God with
us that transcends our understanding or that is yet to be revealed,
but we are spared the absurdity of being deprived by decree of
what is granted by gospel. The New Testament speaks again and
again of mystery: the mystery of the kingdom of God, the mystery
of God's will, the mystery of Christ, the mystery hidden for ages,
the mystery of faith, the mystery of our religion—but, for all that,
Paul, who most used the concept, knows no self-contradicting
God.

> As surely as God is faithful, our word to you has not been Yes and
> No. For the Son of God, Jesus Christ, whom we preached among
> you . . . was not Yes and No; but in him it is always Yes. For all the
> promises of God find their Yes in him. That is why we utter the Amen
> through him, to the glory of God. (II Cor. 1:18–20)

Paul knows the Yes of election, he knows the Yes of the gospel,
he knows the Yes of the appeal "be reconciled to God!" And
he knows the No of judgment on those who are called but will
not repent and believe the gospel. But he knows nothing of the
No of reprobation that countermands what God has affirmed by
denying any possibility of faith and conversion to a whole segment
of humankind. The committee frankly acknowledges this.[1]

1. "Paul, however, does not specifically draw that implication . . ." (p. 538).

The report of the study committee has been referred to the churches as an elucidation of the teaching of election and reprobation in the Canons of Dort. This elucidation includes the brief but radical criticisms found on page 533 of the report. I believe the church should not only take serious note of this, but respond to it constructively. I personally hope to contribute to that response.

Unless I err, some will feel that pursuing and elaborating on the committee's criticisms of Dort may be considered a violation of the Form of Subscription. The final chapter of this book will therefore consider the impasse created by the synods of 1980 and 1981 with respect to credal revision and creative theological writing under the terms laid down in the Form of Subscription.

CHAPTER 6

THE FORM OF SUBSCRIPTION

Before office-bearers in the Christian Reformed Church or professors of Calvin College and Seminary can enter upon the discharge of their duties, and before candidates for the ministry can be ordained, they must sign the Form of Subscription. They do thereby

> sincerely and in good conscience before the Lord, declare by this our subscription that we heartily believe and are persuaded that all the articles and points of doctrine contained in the [Belgic] Confession and [Heidelberg] Catechism of the Reformed Churches, together with the explanation of some points of the aforesaid doctrine made by the National Synod of Dordrecht, 1618-'19, do fully agree with the Word of God.
>
> We promise therefore diligently to teach and faithfully to defend the aforesaid doctrine, without either directly or indirectly contradicting the same by our public preaching or writing.
>
> We declare, moreover, that we not only reject all errors that militate against this doctrine and particularly those which were condemned by the above mentioned Synod, but that we are disposed to refute and contradict these and to exert ourselves in keeping the Church free from such errors. And if hereafter any difficulties or different sentiments respecting the aforesaid doctrines should arise in our minds, we promise that we will neither publicly nor privately propose, teach, or defend the same, either by preaching or writing, until we have first revealed such sentiments to the Consistory, Classis, or Synod, that the same may there be examined, being ready always cheerfully to submit to the judgment of Consistory, Classis, or Synod, under the penalty, in case of refusal, of being by that very fact suspended from our office . . . .[1]

Conformity to the teachings of the three creeds has been so rigorous in the history of the Christian Reformed Church that Dr. John Kromminga in his book *The Christian Reformed Church, A Study in Orthodoxy*, observed the following in connection with a particular heresy trial:

> The Formula of Subscription is again seen as a highly important document with respect to that orthodoxy. What is even more important is the evident willingness of the Christian Reformed Church to apply

1. *Psalter Hymnal*, p. 71

the requirements and threatened punishments of that Formula in a very strict and uncompromising manner.[2]

The ritual of subscription merits serious consideration in the final chapter of this book. Like the Canons, the Form of Subscription was drawn up by the Synod of Dort. It is a document so precise, so airtight, so proof against multiple interpretation that no legal formulation could possibly improve on the absoluteness of all that it requires. Until declarations in the creeds are revised or declared non-binding, the Form of Subscription gives to the creeds a status and authority that in practice stands fully on a level with the Bible itself and not infrequently invites or inspires such interpretation of Scripture as is unwarrantedly supportive of the teaching of the creeds. Any understanding of a teaching in Scripture, however plainly and insistently presented by Scripture, that does not agree with or that contradicts the creeds may become by that fact "unbiblical."

The creeds occupy this position in the CRC in spite of the unambiguous declaration in the Belgic Confession, Article VII, that we may not consider

> any writings of men, however holy these men may have been, of equal value with those divine Scriptures, nor ought we to consider custom, or the great multitude, or antiquity, or succession of times and persons, or councils, decrees or statutes, as of equal value with the truth of God, since the truth is above all . . . .

The statement, therefore, that "all the articles and points of doctrine . . . together with the explanation of some points of doctrine made by the National Synod . . . *do fully agree with the Word of God*" would appear to reflect an unbecoming presumption not only as it stands, but even from the strictly credal point of view.

The strictness and inflexibility with which the Synod of Dort formulated and enforced its creeds was greatly modified in the subsequent church-state relationship. They were retained, however, by the group that seceded from the state church in 1834, and were carried to the United States in the substantial migrations from 1847 on, out of which arose the present Christian Reformed Church. The hold that the Form and its sanctions has on Christian Reformed consistories and church councils, on ministers, pro-

2. Eerdmans, 1949, p. 82

fessors of theology, and professors of Calvin College is incredible. It is so powerful that it need hardly ever be invoked. The threat of its sanctions being effectuated is sufficient to enforce compliance.

There is also another cause of conformity, strictly unofficial, but more significant by far than the occasional heresy trial, which the Form of Subscription ultimately inspires. It is the fear, on the part of ministers and professors, of creating an unfavorable image of themselves. Ministers want to get along with their consistories, councils, and congregations; they also want to remain eligible for calls. Professors in the College and the Seminary want reappointments when they are due, and advancement in academic status and salary. They may have little to fear of fellow faculty members and administration, but the board that governs the College and the Seminary is another matter. The way of wisdom here is not to challenge the tradition in sensitive credal areas. Such, I conceive, are the prudential causes why in matters like reprobation, women in office, higher criticism, and the question of evolution the church receives no instruction to speak of from the ministers and professors of theology, and from the scientifically trained professors in the College.

It is of course most reasonable that office-bearers in the church and teachers in denominationally owned and controlled institutions of learning should sincerely declare adherence to a body of beliefs. The trouble with the signing of the Form of Subscription in the Christian Reformed Church is the manner and spirit in which the signing is required, and the manner and spirit in which the signing is done. The following should be noted:

1. The express purpose of the Form of Subscription is to impose on the church and on the College and the Seminary the imprint of Dort. This imprint is to be derived not only from the Canons as such, but also by understanding the Belgic Confession and the Heidelberg Catechism in the manner in which the Form of Subscription demands. The signer's agreement with the "explanation of some points of the aforesaid doctrine" means that whatever the Belgic Confession and the Heidelberg Catechism may teach about election and reprobation, atonement, the sinfulness of human nature (total depravity), grace, and the perseverance of the saints must be preached and taught in Dortian terms. At no point is the reprehensible character of this requirement so in evidence as in the meaning of Dort for the kind of election that is taught in the Heidelberg Catechism. In it, *Question and Answer* 54 of Lord's Day XXI read as follows:

> Q. What do you believe concerning the *holy catholic church*?
>
> A. That the Son of God, out of the whole human race, from the beginning to the end of the world, gathers, defends, and preserves for Himself, by His Spirit and Word, in the unity of the true faith, a Church chosen to everlasting life; and that I am, and forever shall remain, a living member thereof.

In this statement there is not a breath of reference to reprobation (nor is there any reference to it in any other part of the Catechism); the central object of election is *the church* of which each confesses to be a member; and the whole is wonderfully and comfortingly preachable. This must, according to the Form of Subscription, become permeated with the individualistic election and the massive reprobation theology of the Canons of Dort.

2. This is the *requirement*. This is what the signer solemnly promises to do. What is the *performance*? The performance of this pledged duty is that every office-bearer pays just as little attention to the requirement as he pleases, and the body of office-bearers as a whole pleases strongly to pay no attention to this promise to speak of, once it has been perfunctorily made. The strange conception of compliance with the Form of Subscription in the CRC is this: so long as ministers and professors are silent about their feelings concerning reprobation they are complying with the Form of Subscription. Total absence of criticism of the creeds is taken as total obedience to the Form of Subscription. No unbroken teaching and preaching silence about reprobation year after year will ever be challenged. Diligence in performing all the weighty promises to teach, uphold, and defend it will never be tested or inquired into. Simple silence is compliance. That is the compromise that has been struck in the CRC as between right, center, left, and the two Calvin faculties.

3. Why is it that in spite of the solemn and weighty affirmations and promises made in the signing of the Form of Subscription, in spite of the unambiguous undertakings to defend, teach, preach, and otherwise implement the teachings of Dort, no doctrine in the CRC is more ignored, more silenced, more mortifying, more theologically embarrassing, and more regarded as evangelistically absurd than the doctrine of reprobation?

The reason is simple. It is not believed. Who ever heard a sermon on the "unspeakable consolation" that the "decree of election and reprobation" affords to "pious souls" (Canons, I/6)? What theologian or minister writes instructive and edifying articles about it in the church press? Why does the "Back to God Hour" exclude it from its preaching subject matter? Why has there been not a word of comment on the "elucidating" character of the gravamen study committee report in the church press? Why does that report seek to downgrade the doctrine of reprobation as a decree and as a doctrine by making it an "aspect" and a "facet" of election? Why was it that although the Synod of 1976 gave *carte blanche* to all office-bearers to discuss the issues presented by a gravamen openly and on their merits, not a single professor or minister with any name at all for theological competence (with one exception) wrote either for or against the gravamen? As for the great body of the laity, why was it so silent—if not because the non-instruction that they had received with respect to this doctrine gave them not to know their right hand from their left?

The answer to all these questions is this: because the doctrine of reprobation is not believed. More especially, it is because the doctrine of reprobation is regarded by the great majority of those who have some knowledge in the matter as an ecclesiastical and theological nuisance that all concerned with wish would just go away.

4. So now we have this passing strange and contradictory situation in the Christian Reformed Church:

a. A body of credal theology exists, known as the Canons of Dort, which is not only authoritative in its own right, but which provides the norm for understanding the two earlier creeds, the Belgic Confession and the Heidelberg Catechism.

b. The first and fundamental of these determinative Canons (Head of Doctrine I) sets forth the Reformed teaching on election and reprobation, that is, the positive and the negative, the inclusive and exclusive principles that establish the character of the other Canons.

c. The Form of Subscription requires of all office-bearers and all professors of Calvin College and Seminary the believing and heartfelt adherence to the teaching of the Canons, and of the other two creeds as understood in the light of the Canons; it further requires solemn promises from said subscribers to defend, teach, and otherwise implement these teachings in the church, in which teachings the doctrine of election and reprobation plays the central and basic role insofar as the other two creeds are affected by the Canons.

d. There is exceedingly little reason to believe, and exceedingly much reason to disbelieve, that the co-pivotal companion doctrine of reprobation meets with any significant response of faith and assent in the hearts of the subscribers of the Form. There is consequently every reason to believe, and little reason to disbelieve, that their subscription of this doctrine is a meaningless formality. All this is well known in the broad circles of the informed.

e. No one of all those involved in the signing of the Form of Subscription dares openly to state, least of all in writing, that he or she disbelieves the doctrine of reprobation. Every one, *literally*, is simply silent about it.

f. This universal silence, in full face of the common knowledge, is, *mirabile dictu*,[3] understood by all church assemblies and by all in positions of ecclesiastical authority as fully adequate evidence of complete agreement with, acquiescence in, and faithful execution of those weighty and far-reaching commitments and promises, relative not least to reprobation, the requirement of which constitutues the heart and soul of the Form of Subscription. No one, *but no one*, discerns here the slightest incongruity, the smallest impropriety. On the contrary, upon every due and appropriate occasion all soberly depose, individually and, at the beginning of all synods, collectively, what most heartily detest.

5. How is this mystifying contradiction to be understood? In the considered judgment of this writer the answer lies in the following complex of CRC realities.

The Christian Reformed Church exists ecclesiastically and especially theologically of three parts: a right wing, a center, and a left wing. The center constitutes far more than a majority of the whole. Right and left are fairly constant true minorities. The "right" here does not necessarily mean reactionary, though that element is not wanting in it. By and large, the right wing of the CRC is simply conservative in its approach to just about everything. It stands by the tradition, it looks askance at innovation. It believes in "holding the line." It never has a serious theological question, and it has a plenitude of theological answers for others who do have such questions.

The left wing of the CRC is innovative; its eyes and ears, and its heart, are open to the surrounding world. It is evangelical in word and deed. It is not radical in the accepted political, social, or theological senses of the word. It believes that God has revealed himself not only in the special revelation of Scripture, but also in the general revelation of nature and history. It does not equate

3. A famed Latin saying meaning "wonderful to relate."

these two revelations, however. God's speaking and acting in nature and in history must be seen and understood in the light of redemption as mediated by Christ and his Word. Only in that light can we see light. For these reasons the left does not believe that when in 1619 the Synod of Dort went home the Holy Spirit's guidance of the church into the truth went into retirement.

The center stands in-between these two theologico-ecclesiastical entities. It has points of contact with both wings, tends to agree on this issue with one, on that issue with the other. It moves this-a-way and that-a-way with steadfast unpredictability.

Unfortunately, the good qualities of the left are flawed by a basic defect in its character. It is wanting in that simple quality known as guts. It does not face up to the restrictions on freedom imposed by the Form of Subscription and arbitrarily enforced by the church. It labors at crucial points under a paralysis of will. This paralysis goes so far that it dares not even avail itself of the freedom allowed by the Form of Subscription as revised by the Synod of 1976. The whole church had *carte blanche* for three years to reflect publicly on the doctrine of reprobation as challenged by the gravamen, but, with one or two exceptions, the left utterly failed to do so. There is not the slightest doubt in my mind that ninety percent of the continuing muddle about the "inerrancy" of Scripture itself in the CRC is due to the failure of competent and trusted theological minds among us to lay out before the church the facts of higher criticism. To do this did not even need the revision of 1976. It could have been done readily by bringing Scripture itself to bear on the question in the first place, and further by extensive appeal to acknowledged *evangelical* scholars. But even that was considered too much of a risk for the left.

With a flabby center and a too-cautious left, the right, which can least of all be charged with flabbiness or over-caution in pursuing its "hold-the-line" policy, has been far more influential than either its numbers or its competence warrants. It stands on the rock called the Form of Subscription and calls to severe account those who seem to venture from it. It does so with the amorality characteristic of all subscription. Does it not know that reprobation is disbelieved on all sides? Does it not know that, barring exceptions, it plays no role in the teaching, preaching, pastoral, and apologetic ministry of the Christian Reformed

Church? Other, that is, than making the church's whole ministerial and professorial cadre double-hearted and double-tongued. Assuredly it does. But it is not concerned about this duplicity. What it wants and is content with is *legal conformity* to and a show of *formal compliance with* the Form of Subscription. It is content with public silence on the part of dissenting minds. The center and, in higher degree, the left, while not "content" with this, not only tolerate it but consciously and without protest co-operate with the universal game that keeps the CRC "orthodox."

But this is not all. The power of the right wing rests further, and importantly, in a constant threat that is generally implicit but from time to time verges on the explicit. It is the possibility of secession. This causes the center to tremble and it gives concern to the left. The meeting place of pressure from the right and concession from the center and the left is the manner in which the Form of Subscription is universally regarded and applied. *All* sign it, *all* make believe that *all* the signatories mean exactly the same thing, namely bona-fide loyalty to the unambiguously clear demands of the Form of Subscription, and *all* know that nothing in the whole Christian Reformed Church from New Jersey to Hawaii and from Florida to Alaska is farther from the truth in fact and in spirit.

Such is the vaunted orthodoxy of the Christian Reformed Church on the doctrine of reprobation—a doctrine co-pivotal with election in determining the character of the Canons as a whole. The orthodoxy that is thus maintained is a political orthodoxy in the sense that it is the result of give and take that goes far beyond the legitimate forms of compromise by which all in the church of Christ and indeed in all human society must receive one another. It is an orthodoxy with respect to predestination that is based on fear, insincerity, and violence to conscience, and all this on a massive scale. Scripture calls this "quenching of the Spirit," but the CRC calls it "orthodoxy."

The indifferent formalistic signing of the Form of Subscription must come to an end. The subscription farce may not continue. We must recognize it for what it is—a personal endorsement by hand, in the presence of God and of the church, of a denial of the efficacy of the gospel for an entire segment of the human race.

For the professors of Calvin College and Calvin Seminary the signing is a casual scribble in a big notebook in the office of the College.

If this can continue with the greatest equanimity in the headship of the church and of its academic community, think you, honest reader, that this virus will not infect the entire body? Will not this playing fast and loose with the intentions, promises, and commitments expressed in ordination vows and professional academic obligations ere long influence the value attached to marriage vows, contracts, oaths, engagements, and other undertakings in the life of the laity?

Is there a looser morality for the church leadership than there is for the members? I have always been taught that the moral life of church leaders should be exemplary for the laity, but now in a crucially important area this rule is waived by common consent. This is, however, wholly in keeping with the practice of Christian Reformed synods of being free from law when that is politically convenient.

*   *   *

Finally, a word of serious warning.

The impression that is strongly left by the gravamen study committee report, by the decisions of the Synod of 1980 and their endorsement by the Synod of 1981, is that the doctrine of reprobation is not the mountainous burden that the gravamen presents it as being. It is but an "aspect" or "facet" that is inevitably inherent in the doctrine of election. The great Synod of Dort took note of it "only insofar as was necessary to secure the Reformed doctrine of particular or individual election . . . and to highlight the unmerited grace of election" (p. 522). Presumably, therefore, all may regard and sign the Form of Subscription with complete composure of heart and mind.

Be not deceived. The cosmetic treatment given to the doctrine of reprobation by the Synod of 1980 changed nothing at all in the nature of that old crone. All office-bearers are still required to sign the Form of Subscription and not one word has been changed in that instrument. They will not sign in its stead a codicil known as the gravamen study committee report. Nor will they be required to sign the decisions of the synods of 1980 and 1981.

They will sign *only* the Form of Subscription with its unreserved and iron-clad endorsement of the Dortian doctrine of reprobation. Each of the foregoing synods has made plain that its decisions *in no wise* revised the canonical statement of the doctrine. What all office-bearers in particular and the Christian Reformed Church as a whole continue to affirm, therefore, is

That some receive the gift of faith from God, and others do not receive it, proceeds from God's eternal decree; (I/6)

and that

. . . God, out of his sovereign, most just, irreprehensible, and unchangeable good pleasure, has decreed

a. to leave the reprobate in the common misery into which they have wilfully plunged themselves, and

b. not to bestow upon them saving faith and the grace of conversion; but

c. permitting them in his just judgment to follow their own ways, at last, for the declaration of his justice, to condemn and punish them forever, not only on account of their unbelief, but also for all their other sins. . . . (I/15)

That is what we as a Christian Reformed Church profess to believe about reprobation. All the cosmetic rationalizations by the study committee, all its ignoring of points (a) and (b) above, and its misconstruing of point (c), all the naive approval of the study committee report by the uncomprehending Synod of 1980, and the indifferent endorsement of the Synod of 1980 by the Synod of 1981 change neither jot nor tittle *either* of what Dort says *or* of what the Reformed churches have always believed about reprobation. For the study committee itself, with the approval of two synods, cancels all its clever mitigating theology when at the end of its analysis of the gravamen it writes:

Furthermore, it would seem to be an implication of the teaching of the Canons on reprobation, plus their teaching on the nature of our fallen condition, that for a person who never comes to faith, it was in fact always impossible that he would. (p. 533)

Which, without the softening "seem" and "implication" is what the gravamen stated in the first place.

That, my fellow believers in the Christian Reformed Church, is what you profess to believe. And that, office-bearers in the Christian Reformed Church, is what you affix your seal of sig-

This impressed many as putting God in too harsh a light. Is it compatible with justice to ordain reprobation from all eternity and then use creation and an efficaciously permitted fall to achieve the predetermined end? Should reprobation with all its woeful consequences not arise out of a condition of sin? The more acceptable image of God was achieved by so juggling the pieces of the puzzle that the decree to elect and reprobate came after *(infra)* the fall *(lapsus)*. In this theology, soon to be called infralapsarianism, God first (in order of thought) decreed to create the world and humankind, then he decreed efficaciously to permit the fall; thereupon he made his predestinating decrees relative to humans, and finally decreed to institute the process of salvation in Christ.

This view has a catch in it that deprives it of any claim to have produced a more acceptable image of God than supralapsarian theology gives. Both views determine the eternal fate of all people from the dawn of creation to the end of time as heaven-bound for the elect and hell-bound for the reprobate. Not only were these decrees made before all time, but they fully and absolutely control all people in time. The elect are elect and the reprobate are reprobate solely and exclusively because of God's sovereign good pleasure, which neither saves the elect because of their faith nor reprobates the reprobate because of their unbelief. Seventeenth-century infralapsarianism is as cosmetic a treatment of supralapsarianism as the twentieth-century Christian Reformed study committee report on the reprobation gravamen is a cosmetic treatment of the Canons of Dort. The seventeenth-century practitioners of theological cosmetology were just a bit more professional than their contemporary counterparts. In neither case is the harsh reality of the reprobating decree diminished by even a fraction of a degree.

Basic to the whole supra-infralapsarian discussion there appears to lie a strain of hubris, of human intellectual arrogance, that refuses to be content with the limits imposed on its theological thinking by the data of revelation. It is not satisfied with the revelation of God's grace in Christ and of his power in the destruction of sin and evil. It must also have an explanation of unbelief. It is not willing, according to the divine example, to simply marvel at unbelief (Isa. 5:2c, 3, 4; Mark 6:6a). It must understand it. It wants to penetrate the unrevealed mystery of evil. It is a hubris

that is not willing to entertain the possibility that God himself
does not understand evil, that for that reason his conquest of it
in Christ is revealed, but not its roots. If God cannot make a
square circle can he as the highest rationality comprehend the
deepest irrationality?

Be that as it may, the fascination that the problem of unbelief
has had for Reformed theologians in the context of election has
largely closed their eyes to the revelation of the election of Israel,
of Christ, and of the church. Dort speaks boldly of the reprobation of individuals that has not been revealed, but it has nothing
to say about the election of Israel and it speaks only peripherally
about the election of Christ and of the church, all of which have
been revealed. In trying to close the human-conceived system of
reality it has excluded from its purview elements of the highest
consequence in the divinely conceived system of reality. It is so
enamored of reprobation that it has little eye for God's election
in areas that have no corresponding reprobation associated with
them. Is this in itself not a judgment on the creation of this
doctrine?

The doctrine of reprobation exists only in the Reformed tradition. In that tradition it is inseparably associated with the supra-
infra argumentation. The Canons of Dort I/6 and 15 represent
the infra- emphasis in such a manner that the supra- emphasis is
not prohibited in Reformed churches. The Christian Reformed
synods of 1980 and 1981, while not referring to supra-infra
theology, denied that their endorsement of the study committee
report involved revision of Dort's teaching on reprobation in any
manner. They therefore endorse the kind of thinking that historic
Reformed reprobation theology represents. Of this kind of thinking, specifically as it comes to credal expression, Professor G. C.
Berkouwer has this to say:

> Nowhere, whether in credal formulation or in dogmatic theology, do
> we meet such a problematic complex of difficulties, objections,
> onesidedness, error, and less than correct teaching with respect to the
> official formulation of the doctrine of the church.[1]

2. *Eodem modo*

A second recourse to justify the acceptance of the doctrine of
reprobation is to the denial in the Conclusion of the Canons "that

1. *De Verkiezing Gods* (Kampen, 1955), p. 316. Translation mine.

in the same manner *(eodem modo)* in which the election is the
fountain and cause of faith and good works, reprobation is the
cause of unbelief and impiety.'' The famous statement, usually
designated by its first two Latin words, warrants such acceptance
no more than infralapsarianism does. In repudiating this charge
the Synod of Dort repudiated only a particular *manner* in which
reprobation took place. In no way does this repudiation mean
that the reprobate were not designated as such by the sovereign
good pleasure of God. The accusers of the synod made the mistake
of couching their charge in a theologically defective manner.

The difference between the two manners by which elect became
elect and reprobate became reprobate may be described as the difference between a wholly positive divine action in the former case
and a less positive divine action in the latter. As a result of the
decree to permit Adam to fall all humankind became (in the mind
of God) a common undifferentiated mass of spiritually dead
humanity. Out of this mass God in his decree elected those who
were to be saved as a witness to his mercy and reprobated those
who were to be lost as a witness to his justice. Both the election
and the reprobation arise, as we have seen again and again, out
of God's ''good pleasure,'' that is, without reference to merit or
demerit. The fact that the elect sinned in Adam does not *prevent*
their election; and the fact that the reprobate sinned in Adam does
not *cause* their reprobation.

From this point on, however, the formal as well as the material
ways of elect and reprobate diverge in every respect. God initiated
in his decree a process of implementation to effect the redemption of the elect centering in Christ and involving Israel in the
Old Testament dispensation and the church in the New. Similar
implementation does not exist to effect the eternal death of the
reprobate. They are by God's positive decree of reprobation simply left in the death into which the sin of Adam plunged them,
they are denied the gift of faith and the grace of conversion, and
in the end they are condemned and punished forever.

Such is the technical theological distinction that ''warranted''
the righteous indignation of the synod in repudiating the allega-
tion of those who ''have violated all truth, equity and charity,
in wishing to persuade the public'' of the *eodem modo* charge.